# LEARNING HYPNOSIS

## A COMMON EVERYDAY APPROACH AFTER ERICKSON

ROB MCNEILLY

ISBN: 0995358117

ISBN-13: 978-0-9953581-1-9

**Learning Hypnosis:** A Common Everyday Approach After Erickson /Rob McNeilly

Cover Photo: The mountains of The Isle of Skye in Scotland from The Kyle of Lochalsh by Rob McNeilly.

Cover Design: Natasha Rivers

Tandava Press

www.tandavapress.com

Tandavapress@gmail.com

Printed in the United States of America

This book is offered as a humble gesture of appreciation of my teachers, particularly Milton Erickson, and also to my family however close or distant.

# CONTENTS

# FOREWORD
## BY MICHAEL D. YAPKO, PH.D.

The field of hypnosis is a deeply divided one. Just as the field of psychotherapy is deeply divided – it is said there are more than 500 different forms of therapy in practice today - the field of hypnosis is comprised of many different theoretical perspectives and practical approaches. One can easily see how someone new to the field would be perplexed by the array of perspectives and methods, many of which seem to openly contradict each other. This new book from Dr. Robert McNeilly can help make learning hypnosis a less bewildering endeavor. Dr. McNeilly is a highly experienced clinician and well known teacher of hypnosis who has evolved his own unique perspectives based on the work of the late psychiatrist and innovator, Milton H. Erickson. He presents these in a highly personal, non-academic style that is clear, informative and supportive.

With this book, Dr. McNeilly offers the interested reader some simple ways to think about applying hypnosis, developing the hypnotic relationship, employing hypnotic language, and catalyzing therapeutic changes. The perspectives and methods he advocates are, indeed, simple, but far from simplistic. It takes considerable wisdom to take a subject as complex as hypnosis and distill it down to its essential ingredients. But, Dr. McNeilly does this especially well when he describes the power of compassion, permissiveness, and the language of possibility as the cornerstones of effective hypnosis. He defines the client as the expert on him or herself and unambiguously conveys the respect that he gives to each client's potential to become more. He makes it clear throughout these pages that hypnosis is about creating possibilities and that the power to activate these possibilities belongs to the client. No expert in hypnosis can make someone focus or make someone relax or learn. A skilled practitioner can, however, create an environment that makes it *possible* for the client to choose to focus, relax or learn. In *Learning Hypnosis*, Dr. McNeilly creates an environment that makes it possible for readers to learn ways to not only *do* hypnosis, but *be* hypnotic.

The language of possibility permeates Dr. McNeilly's writing. It is part of his philosophy of treatment, but it is also foundational to his very being. He invites, but doesn't impose. He offers experience, but doesn't tell you that you have to do it his way. He tells stories, but makes his meanings clear. Just as he advocates inviting the client to consider meaningful possibilities in the context of the therapeutic relationship, in these pages he invites the reader to consider the possibilities for learning and using hypnosis.

As you may discover, there are many good reasons to accept these generous invitations.

Michael D. Yapko, Ph.D.
Fallbrook, California
www.yapko.com

# INTRODUCTION

Hello and welcome. My name is Rob McNeilly. I wanted to say something about the context of where this book came from.

Firstly, I like this approach and I notice that others who have learnt it, like it. It tends to create an experience of possibility and flexibility in clients and this allows a smoother, respectful, and often quicker resolution of their suffering. As a side benefit, we have the benefit of being part of creating an increased personal and professional satisfaction. If we work in a fish market, sooner or later we will smell of fish and, if we work with flowers …

Secondly, I notice that we all feel more alive when we are contributing to something greater than our own petty ego. As a child, I loved our family pets - dogs, cats, chickens, even a cockatoo. When I was in medical practice, the experience of seeing a baby come into this world, a small child getting over an illness, a man or woman begin to heal after an injury, an old person find that they are going to survive a crisis or die peacefully - so many experiences like these were nourishment for my soul.

Thirdly, I have always liked exploring. As a teenager, I was interested in Yoga, the Rosicrucians, the origin of the universe, anything on the fringe of the usual. Jay Haley said that hypnosis hangs out with marginal people.

Perhaps most importantly, I learnt to love freedom and expansiveness. When a teacher says that a child will never make it; when a doctor uses his authority to restrict someone in their care by telling them that they are going to die in three months, that they are incurable or that they will always be mentally ill, something fires up in me and makes me hopping mad.

When a teacher encourages a child to expand their view of what may be possible; when a doctor uses their authority to have the possibility of reducing their suffering or even being cured, my heart lifts.

Heinz von Foerster's ethical imperative to always act to increase options resonates with who I am.

*A woman wanted help because she was feeling increasingly shy with other people. After several sessions she was feeling more confident. As she was leaving, she confided that after her first child, she had a psychotic breakdown. When I asked what she meant by that, she said that she had lost touch with reality. She had no family support, including from her husband, and she became totally overwhelmed. I reminded her about a commotion during our first session with fire trucks and police cars where a house had burnt to the ground. When I told her that it was caused by an electric blanket catching fire, and regretted that it hadn't blown a fuse, she became interested. When I asked her if she had had a psychotic breakdown or blown a fuse, she became very thoughtful. She then said that she was angry that she had been given the burden of "psychotic breakdown" and looked pleased and optimistic when I asked her about what she might do if she felt overwhelmed in the future. She seemed relieved when she said she would blow a fuse. I didn't see her again, so I don't know if she blew any more fuses or had more "psychotic breakdowns," but from her response to our short conversation I am confident her future was more within her influence.*

Some background.

I had a medical training and was in a suburban family medicine practice in Melbourne, Australia, for 10 years. It was wonderful to be a part-time member of so many families with their suffering, their illnesses and their troubles and to be able to support and help them.

One of the outstanding joys was the amazing experience of being present and helping the delivery of hundreds of babies. It was a highlight of my medical practice. And, while I really enjoyed that work, while I really enjoyed contributing to people and helping to support them with their physical problems and their troubles, I found that I was completely inadequately prepared to deal with their human dilemmas. When someone had some emotional problem, when they were frightened unnecessarily, when they were depressed or worried unnecessarily, when they had physical pain, the best I could do was offer some tablets.

This deficit led me to explore hypnosis. My initial introduction was through a very traditional approach where I learnt that hypnosis was something you needed to be very careful of, since it was special and dangerous. This meant that a lot of training was required so the special skills could be learnt before you could even begin.

I learnt a formula. You ask someone to look at a spot, ask them to relax their toes and progressively relax the rest of their body. You then tell them that their eyes are getting heavier, they are getting sleepy, they're going to close their eyes. And then, when that happened, to issue instructions: "You won't do that, you will do this. In future, you won't be able to have the problem. Instead, you will have this solution - one resulting from my special understanding." It was like a psychic operation in which the hypnosis was an anesthetic where you put someone out, put them under, put them to sleep, make them unconscious so you could do the psychic surgery and excise the problem.

I noticed that this was very effective with some people, but there were others who didn't take to it and, in my ignorance, I labeled these people as being resistant, not ready, not willing, having secondary gain, completely missing the fact that it was my incompetence that was causing the stuckness.

I was also bored, using the same repetitious patter, hour after hour. Sometimes I even had trouble staying awake.

All of this changed when I had the great fortune and privilege of hearing about Milton Erickson, seeing Herb Lustig's wonderful film of him working The Artistry of Milton H Erickson MD and then, in the last few years of his life, meeting him, spending some time with him, getting to know him and be known by him, learning directly from him. What I learnt in my time with Erickson revolutionised my approach to hypnosis and had a massive influence over the effectiveness of what I was able to offer.

Erickson assumed that people had resources. He assumed that each person was the expert, knew more about themselves than they realised, more than we could ever know. This shifted the focus from me as having to pretend to be an expert, to the role of helping the client to regain their expertness. It was like my experience in general practice of helping women to deliver their babies. I didn't need to be an expert at pregnancy. I'd never been pregnant, never likely to be pregnant. My job was to do whatever I could to allow the process of giving birth to be as natural and as unimpeded as possible so that the natural process could just run its course.

This then became my job as a therapist - to help remind the client they have the capacity, help them to find a way of connecting with that capacity, reconnecting with preferred experiences so that they could have access to them. My job was to generate a mood of expectancy and trusting, of lightness, of possibility. It revolutionised my attitude to hypnosis, which became so much more effective and enjoyable. Instead of being wrung out and bored at the end of the day, I frequently felt enlivened.

And like any experience that we enjoy, that we are taken by; any experience that we find touches us, I began to share this experience with others. And over the last 35 years or so, I've been offering workshops face to face in different parts of the world and, more recently, online, helping to share this approach, my version of what Erickson did … my expression of what I learnt from my time with this man. A lot of people have told me that they find that learning this approach, learning in this way, is of huge benefit to their practice and to their person.

In writing this book, I'm offering a guide so that as a reader, you can have an opportunity to see what might be useful, to see what might be helpful to explore, to adapt, to translate. I want to emphasise that I am not in any way claiming that what this book is about is the right, the best, the only way of doing something. It is simply offered as my observation of my experience so that anyone reading it can try it out, use it, adapt it or even do the opposite of what I'm suggesting here.

After more than 30 years, I am increasingly enchanted by what Erickson's approach makes available. My appreciation has only expanded over time ... and that is me and my experience.

My invitation to you is to enjoy your reading of what I've written, what I've shared, then to use it, to change it, to throw it out, or do anything that can be useful for you and your learning. I'm very grateful to have the opportunity to share this work and I'm very grateful for you to take the time and read it with the possibility of adding to your effectiveness and your personal satisfaction.

# Section 1
## Demystifying Hypnosis - Principles

### Principles

Hypnosis has kept very strange company over the years. It's been associated with magic, with sorcery, with the devil, with anaesthesia. And, if we look at the way magicians do their magic, magicians are characteristically charismatic male figures, who appear and make very dramatic gestures so that they can work their magic on some passive recipient.

This association with magic lives on, where stage hypnotists are very powerful, charismatic creatures, usually male, who do weird things to some passive recipients, who feel compelled to surrender to the will and the strength of the stage hypnotist.

This also persists in traditional approaches to hypnosis in which the hypnotist, usually a male, takes on a very commanding position, is an expert. And with great authority, tells their subject, "You are doing this! You will get sleepy! You will close your eyes!"

There was a wonderful expression of this in an old black and white movie of Dracula where Dracula was confronting Van Helsing, who had caught up with him. Dracula, who was played by a Hungarian opera singer, Bela Lugosi, stands there with his black cape and piercing eyes, looks directly into Van Helsing's eyes, makes gestures and says very dramatically, "Come ... come!"

It's rather amusing as we see Van Helsing looking a little confused and quite close to submitting to the power of Dracula's hypnotic gaze, but managing to shake himself out of it and regain his own autonomy. Dracula replies by saying, "You have a very strong will!"

It's rather quaint, but this idea of a hypnotist, even a hypnotherapist having to have a stronger will and overpower the weaker, passive subject is still, unfortunately persisting.

Sorcery is rather different. In sorcery, the power of sorcery is in the spells. You can go into any new age book shop and buy a book of spells. It's then simply a matter of the person wanting to use the spells to speak the words. The power is in the words. It has nothing to do with the speaker. Anyone can do it. All that's needed is to speak the words perhaps with some ritual, with chicken feet. The sorcery happens from the power of the words that affect some passive, perhaps not even aware victim, who then is taken over by the power of the words of the spell.

To my regret, this still persists in a lot of hypnotic work in the form of hypnotic scripts where the person comes in for hypnosis and the therapist says, "What's the problem?"

When the client says, "I've got a problem with this, that or the other ... I can't sleep or I've got pain," the therapist finds a book of hypnotic scripts, looks up the scripts and then simply, having put the client into a hypnotic state, reads the scripts as if the scripts have the power.

It might be relevant to have a standard script, if we could find a standard person. In all my years as a doctor and a therapist, I haven't met one yet. So there's a very severe limitation that comes from relying just on rigid scripts and the power of their words.

Another association that hypnosis has is with general anaesthetics. Both became popular just over 100 years ago and a lot of the jargon of general anaesthetics has crept over into the jargon of hypnosis so that, in a lot of hypnotic circles, there is talk of putting someone to sleep, putting them out, putting them under, making them unconscious so then the person will be unaware of what's happening.

As with a general anaesthetic, there are fears. Will it work? There's nothing worse than having an operation when the anaesthetic doesn't work. Another concern is will I wake up? Will I be permanently entranced in the same way that there is a worry about anaesthesia - will I wake up at all?!! Also, there is a worry about will I say something that I'll later regret? Will I behave badly? These concerns, in relation to hypnosis are a direct result of the fallacious connection between hypnosis and general anaesthetic.

Hypnosis then still evokes a popular response of being overpowering, of being overpowered, of loss of control, and so, fear. It's regarded as a special way of working in therapy. In Australia, there are still some insurance companies that require a higher premium for a therapist using hypnosis, presumably because of the additional danger that goes with something so powerful as hypnosis. In Australia, some states, until recently, had very strict restrictions on who could or who could not use hypnosis. Fortunately, these absurd restrictions are now becoming redundant.

I like to joke with people learning hypnosis with me that, if they were to meet some of their friends and say to their friends, "I'm learning about hypnosis," to see their friends' response. The response can often be absurd, even from an otherwise intelligent person, who looks away and says, "Don't do that. Are you doing that to me now? Don't look at me that way," as if they are terrified of being taken over by the "hypnotic gaze."

Hypnosis is not then a way of overpowering someone. It's not a way of controlling them. It's not a function of the power of the therapist. It's not a function of the power of the words. It has nothing to do with being unconscious.

What then is hypnosis? I have found, in all the years I've been exploring this that there is no satisfactory agreement amongst experts about what hypnosis really is.

Freud used hypnosis all those years ago and gave it up for free association and likened hypnosis to falling in love. Erickson said that, for him, hypnosis was a special form of communication between client and therapist. And both of them emphasised the relational aspect, which points to one of the marvellous benefits of using hypnosis.

## WHAT IS HYPNOSIS, REALLY?

I have found that rather than trying to define hypnosis, which can tie it down in some rigid way, it is more useful to give a description so that when we use the word, we can have some agreement about what we mean.

For me, it can be a relief to think of hypnosis as

>an experience
>
>where there is focus
>
>and absorption
>
>that we can mutually agree as being "hypnosis."

By having this description and emphasising the experiential aspect of hypnosis, by identifying the components of focus and absorption and particularly by emphasising that it is only hypnosis by mutual agreement, we can avoid debating about what hypnosis really is and what it really isn't.

It follows for me that we can think of meditation as an experience where there's focus and absorption that we call meditation; mindfulness as an experience with focus and absorption that we can call mindfulness, EMDR or TFT as experiences with focus and absorption that we can call EMDR or TFT. There are differences between these approaches in what the focus is, and we can also see the similarities between these experiences so we don't have to get involved in complex arguments about whether meditation, mindfulness, EMDR or TFT is the same as hypnosis or different from it.

We can then begin to explore hypnosis and how someone can go into hypnosis, based on this description. All we need to do is to find a way of helping a person to have an experience, to become focused and to become absorbed in that experience. This allows us a much simpler approach. We don't then have to learn complex techniques or convoluted methods of hypnotic "induction." We can simply invite anyone interested into an experience, invite some focus, invite some absorption and then invite the possibility of this being called hypnosis.

From this perspective, we can get to the usefulness of hypnosis without having to be bogged down by all of the minutiae and arguments about what it is or isn't, really. This allows hypnosis to be much more ordinary, much more a common everyday experience and brings it out of the weirdness, out of the ivory tower complexity of some special theoretical position.

We can begin to explore, with each individual client, what experience would be useful for them, how they could benefit from focusing and becoming absorbed in it so that they can move from their problem and towards their solution.

## THE COMMON EVERY DAY TRANCE

One of the things I appreciate about Erickson is his linking of hypnosis with the common everyday trance where we can be reading a book, watching a movie, listening to music, walking in nature. There can be focus, there can be absorption. We're not calling this hypnosis, and if anyone were to look, it would be apparent that there are multiple examples of this in our everyday life.

If you are interested, it's simply a matter of looking at friends or family in their ordinary, everyday experiences when they're watching television, when they're looking out of the window, daydreaming, when they're gardening and absorbed in some activity. You can also look at examples with your colleagues, friends, family, strangers or within yourself when we are engaged in some activity and to observe the focus and absorption in such an experience.

Because the common everyday trance is so common, so every day, and because every person has an ability, in their own way, to focus on something and become absorbed in it, we don't need to be sidetracked with the question of whether someone can be hypnotised or not; whether someone is a suitable subject for hypnosis.

I've been asked many times, "What are the requirements for someone to go into hypnosis?" And I like to reply, "They need to be breathing." I've noticed that any person, who is alive has the capacity to focus on something, become absorbed in that something and so we can have the ingredients for any individual to go into hypnosis, not in some formulaic way, but in a way that's particular to them, to their individuality, to their uniqueness.

We can then put aside questions of "Can I be hypnotised?" measurements of hypnotisability, worries about "depth" of trance, since in our individual experiences of everyday trance, our degree of focus and absorption varies. We can be deeply absorbed in reading a fascinating book, and if the phone rings, we put the book aside, answer the phone and then return to the book naturally and easily.

It's then simply up to us to find ways of helping a client to find something useful and relevant to focus on and become absorbed in, rather than to test them to see if they can be hypnotised.

## EASY INVITATIONS

When I first learnt hypnosis, I had to learn specific, rigid hypnotic induction techniques … "Look at that spot, relax your body, your eyes are getting sleepy, they are going to close …" And while this was often effective, it was very boring, hour after hour, using the same words, the same technique. I had trouble staying awake at times.

Also, some people didn't respond to these suggestions. They couldn't continue to look at the spot that I asked them to look at. They found that when they tried to relax their body, they just got tense. And sometimes their eyes weren't getting sleepy. Sometimes their eyes didn't close. Then we were in big trouble. Usually the way I managed this, in my ignorance, was to say that they were resistant, had secondary gain, weren't ready to change, or that they were poor hypnotic subjects, that hypnosis was not suitable for them.

Since my learning with Erickson, I prefer to invite someone to experience something, and then invite them to begin to focus on some aspect of that experience and allow a natural absorption to follow. In response to such an invitation, nothing is imposed, there is no intrusion. Each individual can find their own focus, their own degree of absorption, adding to their senses of autonomy and self-trust.

I can then comment on any physiological changes that can be observed and that we want to encourage.

I have noticed that when anyone begins to focus and become absorbed in an experience, no matter what it is, there is a natural tendency for their breathing to change, however subtly, usually becoming a little slower and a little deeper. There is often an alteration in their blinking, usually slowing down, and sometimes with an interesting tendency for the eyelids to remain closed for just a minutely longer amount of time, almost like their eyelids become a little sticky, just reluctant to open - very subtle. But I've noticed that if we look for it, we can often see it.

Also it's common to be able to observe a flattening out of the facial muscles, a smoothing out of the face, sometimes the shoulders lower. Some astute observers can also notice, at times, a slowing of the pulse that's visible in the neck. Oft times, there is a relative stillness in the body in adults, although children, of course, have their own way of becoming focused and absorbed. Often, they keep moving quite noticeably. But in adults, usually there's some stillness.

If we comment on these observable changes, there's a tendency for those changes to be enhanced, which ratifies to the client that something is happening and, as well as that, adding to the therapeutic relationship, since the client feels respected and their experience is affirmed.

As well as commenting on the specific changes, we can make generic comments as background reassurance and encouragement, by saying things like, "that's good," "that's right," "ah-ha," "good," "yes," "lovely," "fine." It's not a matter of commenting on everything - just what we want to encourage. If a client is fidgeting, we don't need to comment on that, although we could perhaps say, "I notice that there's a lot of stillness in your feet."

Inviting someone in this way into a focused, absorbed experience that is their experience, and having their experience validated and enhanced, is a much more respectful and effective approach than applying some rigid hypnotic induction technique.

## Continue Doing What You're Doing

If we ask a client, a friend, or if you're interested to try, yourself, to continue doing whatever they are doing – it might be looking at you, looking out of the window, noticing their own breathing, listening to some music – whatever it is that they happen to be doing, and then, as they continue doing that, to invite them to have a natural focus and then, as a natural consequence, to allow an increased absorption, all this happening naturally and easily.

If we then observe the client's obvious physiological changes that accompany any experience of focused absorption, then we can comment on these: the slowing of their breathing, their eyelids blinking differently, smoothing out of their face, relative stillness, etc. ... Commenting on these helps to enhance these changes as natural.

Since a client is already doing what they're doing, there is no need to have the question of whether they can or not, given that they're already doing it. And since the focus and absorption is a natural consequence, the whole process tends to be smooth, easy and respectful. We're not suggesting anything; merely inviting such a client into their own individual experience, into their own individual way of focusing, their own individual experience of becoming absorbed and, as such, because it is an experience with focus and absorption, we can then call this hypnosis.

Some clients will come asking specifically for hypnosis. So it will be important to be explicit and say, "This is what we mean by hypnosis." If we don't do that, they'll be dissatisfied. On the other hand, if someone doesn't like the idea of hypnosis, we don't need to mention the H-word. We can simply invite an experience, focus and absorption and we can do this with total integrity because we're not pretending that it's not hypnosis. We're not trying to con someone into having hypnosis when they don't realise because, in this approach, we are saying that hypnosis is only hypnosis when it's mutually agreed to be hypnosis.

## DOING SOMETHING YOU LIKE

When any of us do something that we enjoy, that we like to do, we have all of the resources right at our fingertips, ready to deal with any hiccups, disruptions and problems. If someone likes riding their bicycle, they are ready to adapt to hills, weather, punctures, their chain coming off, falling off and so on. These occurrences are treated as temporary interruptions. They're taken care of and then the cycling continues. If such a person wasn't able to manage these problems easily, they would hardly continue to like cycling. The fact that they like it means they've got it handled.

If someone likes gardening, they'll be ready to adapt to dirt under their fingernails, scratches from thorns, the experience of pruning, the fact that some plants die. These occurrences, again, are simply temporary interruptions in the total experience of doing something that they like to do.

So, if we ask a client to recall or imagine that they are doing something that they like to do, they not only like to do what they like to do, but they like to experience it. And most people will be very willing, even keen, to allow themselves the experience of recalling or imagining something that they like to do.

Then, having started by inviting them to do something they like to do, we can invite them to begin to focus on some part of the experience, something of their choosing, and then, as a natural consequence of that focusing, to allow themselves to become more absorbed to whatever degree they are becoming absorbed. Then all we need to do, as before, is to comment on any of the associated physiological changes, the changes in their breathing, their blinking, the smoothing out of their face, stillness in their body, etc..

We then have all the ingredients of a hypnotic experience, one that is a function of the individual; not imposed by us, and as a bonus, one that is full of resources.

## WHAT'S WRONG? OR WHAT'S MISSING?

How can we move from a problem-solving approach to a solution-generating approach?

When I was in medical practice, someone would come in as a patient with their problem. And, if I were to do my job as a good doctor, I would ask them, "Tell me about what's happening and when did it start, where is the pain?" I wanted to know all of the facts, all of the information that so then I could make a diagnosis. Then, having made the diagnosis, comes the treatment.

If we have a problem with our car, we take it to a car mechanic and he says, "What's the problem?" He listens to noises, bumps, squeaks, things that are not working. He gets the information and finds as much as he can so that he can find out what's wrong with the car so that, if something needs replacing or fixing, he can do that. If something goes wrong with our washing machine or with our computer, we take it to someone who knows how to fix these things and they either ask, "What's happening, what's wrong, what's not working properly?" or they go about testing, in their own way, perhaps with some special equipment, to find out what is wrong, what's not working, what's broken. And then they fix it, they tighten it, they replace it or they say, "It can't be fixed. Throw it away and get another one."

This problem-solving approach is excellent for dealing with physical problems in the human body, with cars, with computers, with any mechanical object, by finding out what's wrong, making a diagnosis and then fixing it.

Many contemporary approaches to psychological problems are based on the medical model, as if the body is a machine that needs maintenance and then, if something's not working, needs to be fixed.

This idea has percolated across to our thinking and our feeling so that many psychological approaches are mechanistic. We talk about depression, as if something is being pressed down. We talk about being stressed or being distressed. There's a lot of mechanically informed jargon that finds its way into therapy. It's my experience that, although finding techniques to help fix mechanistic processes is wonderful, they are not so good. They don't work so well when it comes to human dilemmas and psychotherapy.

Milton Erickson said, "Clients come to therapy not because of their unchangeable past, but because of some discontent in their present and a desire to better their future" so his approach to therapy was not to find out information about the past so that someone could be treated or fixed, but rather to explore what might be helpful for them so that they could move towards their desired future.

He told me that a woman rang him, saying she wanted some help because she'd been washing her hands obsessively for 12 years. He said he was very interested to find out what she used to do with her hands 13 years ago. He was not interested in diagnosing the problem. He was not interested in getting an understanding of what caused it. He was more interested in helping her to reconnect with some personal resource to create the kind of present, the kind of future that she wanted.

This speaks to the very different approach that Erickson generated and that people who have learnt from him, appreciate. I call this the solution approach. In the solution approach, we are not so much interested in information about causes, but more in gathering information about what resource, what experience that this particular client has become disconnected from, is overlooking, is not making use of or could learn.

In the problem-solving approach, the whole process is informed by the question, "What's wrong that needs fixing?" In the solution approach, it's informed by the question, "What's missing?" What's missing that, if this client were able to find it, connect with it, access it, learn it, that they would be okay. The whole process in the solution approach, rather than being concerned with fixing, is primarily concerned with connecting. It's informed not by what's wrong, but it's informed by what's missing.

"What's missing?" is such a beautiful question that, if we have it in the background, helps to give a direction, helps to give us a format for exploring with each individual client just what it is that's going to be useful for them, helpful to them to move towards their preferred future.

There are a couple of marvelous Irish sayings. One is, "If you don't know where you're going, you might end up in a different place." Another variation of that is, "If you don't know where you're going, any road will take you there." If we know where we're going, if we can find the direction that's going to be useful for the client, then that's going to be so helpful in giving direction to the whole therapeutic approach.

To summarise, the problem-solving approach is informed by the question, "What's wrong that needs fixing?" It involves categorising and treating while the solution approach is informed by the question, "What's missing?" What has the client become disconnected from so that we can assist them to connect, to reconnect or to learn so that they can be enabled to get on with their life, resolve their conflict and have the preferred future that they want?

# Section 2
## Designing a hypnotic session

We've already seen how respectful and easy it can be to invite someone into a focused, absorbed experience. We know how easy it is when this experience is something that someone likes to do. We've also explored how, what's missing for the client, what it is that we are going to look for with them is predictably present in their likes, in something that they like to do.

This leads to a process where it can be natural, easy and respectful for a client to look within the experience of being focused and absorbed in something that they like and find precisely the resource that is missing in their problem. It's such a joy to be part of this experience and it still touches me how precise and predictable this connection can be.

So here is a format, not one that I'm recommending that you use strictly, but rather one that I invite you to practice, to play with, to explore, so that you can make your own variations and spend more time on one part or another, add some extra steps, leave some steps out and make your own version of it.

Here's the format that I want to offer so that you can vary from it.

before hypnosis
likes? likes?
problem? problem?
what's missing

— — — — — — — — — — —

during hypnosis
go to likes - focus & absorb then comment
look for missing resource
learn it
bring it to the problem

— — — — — — — — — —-

after hypnosis
what's different?
completing the session

## WHAT DO YOU LIKE?

Erickson told me, "When a client comes to see you, they always bring the solution with them, only they don't know that they bring their solution with them, so have a very nice time talking with clients, helping them to find the solution that they brought with them that they didn't realise they brought." When I first heard that, I thought it was charming. I really liked it, but I was left with the dilemma: how do you do that? And since I've been exploring each individual client's likes that the pieces have started to come together.

We can begin a session by asking a client, "What do you like to do?" By simply putting that question, clients find themselves, in responding to it, in a resourceful state. Most people like talking about what they like to do and it's a delight to be with someone who comes in heavy with the problem, and ask them what they like to do and see their eyes start to shine, a smile on their face, a lift in their mood. There's a very different person present, simply in response to that question. We can safely assume that because a client likes something, they must have all the resources that they need right at their fingertips to handle any disruption, any minor hiccups, otherwise they wouldn't like it.

If someone, for example, likes cycling, that doesn't mean they'll never have a puncture, the chain won't come off, they won't fall off, they won't have problems with the weather and so on. It means that they have the resources that they need to handle those minor interruptions and, because they have the resources, they can continue cycling and continue liking it. If they didn't have the resources, then they wouldn't continue liking it.

## What Do You Like About That?

The next step is to clarify, "What is it that you like about it?" We, and the client can discover the unique deep connection they have with this activity. It's so enlightening, so helpful for us and sometimes it's a discovery for a client to hear their own response to that question. If someone likes cycling and we ask them, "What do you like about that?" some people will like the exercise. Some people will like being out in the open air. Some people will like cycling because they get away from something - they're on their own, while other people will like cycling because they can cycle with their friends – or be with others as a way of connecting! So, until we find out what someone likes about their likes, we can only guess and we are likely to ascribe what we would like about that, completely missing what the client likes, which is the crucial aspect to know about.

When we ask someone what they like about what they like doing, it's like a window into their soul. We have a very intimate glimpse into who this person is at core and often that glimpse is not only for us. Sometimes the client is so touched by that that it can make a huge difference, just to make that connection.

## WHAT'S THE PROBLEM?

The next step is to look at the problem. Clients come with problems and, if we just keep talking about what they like to do, they're hardly going to be satisfied. So we can ask a client, "What is the problem?"

Groucho Marx was two hours late for a speaking arrangement and when asked why he was so late, he replied that on his way to the event, someone asked him how his family was, so he told them.

Instead of asking "What's the problem?" we can ask, "What could we talk about here that would be useful? If something could happen today that would be beneficial for you, what would that be?" This is a way of asking the client about the problem that is not just asking for details about how the problem actually is; it's a way of asking about the problem that, in the asking, helps to move the client towards a resolution.

When we ask, "What could we talk about today that would be helpful to you?" it creates the possibility of help. Saying, "If we could do something that would be useful for you," introduces the possibility of usefulness. If we ask, "If we had a conversation today that was really helpful to you that made a big difference and you said that you were okay, what would that be?" Just being present to that question introduces a direction and a possibility of the client being okay, sometimes for the first time.

## WHAT'S THE PROBLEM ABOUT THE PROBLEM?

Just as asking what someone likes about their likes can be so helpful, asking a client, "In what way is this problem problematic to you?" can also be very helpful in clarifying for us and for the client just what it is that we need to attend to. If someone has a problem because of a past trauma, for example, if we don't ask, "In what way is this still problematic to you?" then we are left with the only option of treating PTSD. But, if we asked, "What part of this trauma is still worrying you or still troubling you?" then we might hear, "I get flashbacks," "I can't sleep," "I don't feel good about myself," "I've got too much pain," or it might be, "I can't work and I feel bad about not being able to support my family."

When we explore this second step, it helps to clarify what's missing for a client, which is going to be helpful when we go looking for it.

If someone is having a problem in trauma with flashbacks, then we're going to be working with an experience of helping someone to resolve the past, maybe to have less attention or forget some of the trauma or to have a different response to it so that either the flashbacks stop or are less troublesome.

If someone has trouble sleeping, then we'll be dealing with how to help someone go to sleep or stay asleep or get back to sleep or to wake up feeling refreshed.

If someone isn't feeling good about themselves, then we'll be working with their issues of self-esteem. If someone is feeling bad because they can't support their family, then we'll be looking for other ways of accepting the change or exploring alternative ways of supporting the family.

Obviously, if we don't ask for the specifics, whatever we do is likely to percolate across to all areas of this client's life. But if we ask specifically what it is about this problem for this particular client that is problematic, that allows us to focus more effectively, more respectfully, in a shorter time, leading to a more lasting resolution and so we are going to be more helpful for this client.

## WHAT'S MISSING?

It may be enough, when we find out about what the problem is and how come that's a problem. It might become apparent where to go from there. If someone says, "I can't go to sleep," then we know what's missing for them is likely to be going to sleep. But it can also be very helpful at times to ask specifically if it's not clear, to explore with them, "What is it that's missing for you? What is it that, if you were to have access to it, you would be okay?"

Different ways of getting some clarification about what's missing for a client, apart from simply asking directly, "What's missing?" is to ask a miracle question. "If a miracle happened and, while you were asleep tonight, the problem resolved, you'll wake up in the morning and, because that resolution happened while you were asleep, you don't know what it was, but you wake up, the problem's gone. What's different?" And, if we listen to whatever the client says is different when they wake up in the morning and the problem's gone this will give us a clue from what's present in their experiences of their resolution and to what is missing or absent in the problem.

We can ask, "If you were to have some therapy here and at the end of that last session, you say, 'I don't need to see you anymore,' what would be different?" This is another future-paced question that takes the client to the experience beyond the problem to when it's been resolved, to look at what's different then. And again, if we listen to what's different at the end of therapy, it gives us a very good clue about what is missing at the beginning of therapy.

These questions all help to clarify for the client and for us what's missing so that then we know what to look for with greater precision, how to explore their experience and in their likes, where we know the resource will be, to be clearer about exactly what it is we're looking for so we have a better chance of finding it.

Now that we have some clarity about what's missing for each individual client, and we know where to look for it, the stage is set. We're ready for respectful and easy hypnosis so that the client has a chance to allow their own unique solution to emerge through making their own unique connections from within their own unique experiences.

When I first began this work, I usually spent the first session gathering as much information as I could - full name, address, date of birth, place of birth, place in the family, educational experience, when the problem began, what made it worse, what helped, what treatment had already been tried, etc., etc., etc., so that when they came for their second session I'd have all the information I needed. The problem was that, because of my poor handwriting, I couldn't read some of my notes, and the client's experience had changed in the interim!

Now I prefer to gather just enough information to make a beginning - what do you like, what do you like about that, what's the problem, what is it about that that's a problem to you, what's missing ... and start from there.

Rather than detailed historical notes, I prefer to record words, phrases, metaphors that each client uses so I can remind myself to include these in our conversations. This creates an experience for each client that we are speaking their language, which we are, adding to the quality of the relationship.

I have found that if we can make a start, and create a helpful experience, however small, that the client can leave with a solid sense of accomplishment which sets up future learning opportunities with us or independent of us.

So let's begin ....

During hypnosis

Go to likes - focus & absorb then comment

Look for missing resource

Learn it

Bring it to the problem

**During Hypnosis**

### INVITATIONS INTO HYPNOSIS

We've explored the way we can think of hypnosis as an experience that involves focus and absorption that we mutually agree as being hypnosis. We've also explored how easy it is for any person to become focused and absorbed in something that they like to do. So it makes perfect sense then, as a way of inviting someone into a hypnotic experience that would be useful to them and relevant to them, to invite them into an experience that they like and to then invite focus and absorption so that we can have what we can agree on as a hypnotic experience.

We can ask someone, "Would it be okay for you to do something that you like to do?" Of course, the client has already told us what that is. So, if they like reading a book, we can say, "Would it be okay to read a book?" If they like walking in nature, we can ask, "Would it be okay to go walking in nature?" If they like to cycle, "Can we go for a bike ride?" And, because we all like to do something that we like to do, when we invite someone into the experience of doing something they like to do, we can expect that that would be very agreeable and easy.

We can offer alternatives, like, *"You might like to remember some specific time, just recently or sometime in the past, or some imagined time that didn't really happen. It really doesn't matter. And then, as you allow yourself to connect with this experience of doing something that you like to do, to allow yourself to begin to focus on some part of your experience, and you may find yourself focusing on one particular aspect of it or you might notice that your focus shifts from here to there, to different places, different parts of the experience. None of that's important. You might even find that you start focusing on one experience and then find yourself becoming more interested in another experience. So all you need to do is allow yourself to focus in whatever way you are focusing on, whatever part of your experience that you find yourself focusing on."*

Then we can invite this client... *"You can become more absorbed. As a part of any experience of focusing, it's only natural to allow yourself to become more absorbed in the experience, and so, as it continues, that absorption can increase and it doesn't need to increase in a way that you might expect or that you might think that I want, but you can simply allow the absorption to increase in any way that it does."*

Next, we can comment on the various changes. If we look for them, they're often very apparent. We can look at the breathing and comment on what we very frequently and expectedly find. *"Your breathing is showing those subtle changes. It's slightly slower, slightly deeper."* We can talk about the blinking. *"I noticed that your blinking is showing those interesting alterations, a little bit slower and of maybe a very faint hint of pausing before they open each time."* We can comment on the facial configuration. It's very common for someone in any focused, absorbed experience to find that their facial muscles are smoothing out.

Predictably, we can expect some stillness [except for children]. In adults, if there is some stillness, we can comment on this. *"There's a lot of immobility in your body. And, although you know you could move, perhaps for the time, you really don't need to move, but can allow yourself to be comfortably still."*

Speaking about these changes that we can observe helps to ratify for each client that something is happening. Also, as we speak about them, there is a tendency for these experiences to be enhanced. If for example, we're looking for stillness and there's fidgeting in someone's hands, we don't need to mention that. We can just say, *"I notice that your feet are very still."*

These observations need to be pure observations without any interpretation. If we say, *"You are comfortably still,*" that's a presumption on our part. We don't know whether someone's comfortable or not. All we can do is comment on what we can observe. Some people may look relaxed, but may not feel relaxed. It's best to keep our observations to simple observable facts, devoid of any interpretation or meaning that may or may not fit with the individual client's experience.

When such a client has an opportunity to begin to focus and then become absorbed in some experience that they like, we can encourage them to pay attention to the different senses as they become aware of by asking questions about each of the senses in turn. *"What can you see, if you look to the left, to the right, if you look above, if you look behind you? Who else is there?"* We can ask about sounds, *"Is there anything in particular that you become aware of, any sounds around?"*

We can ask, *"Is there anything in the air? Can you smell something?"* Some people will notice the freshness in the air or the saltiness of the sea spray if they're walking by a beach. We can ask anyone, *"Is there any particular taste in your mouth?"* This is not very often fruitful, but it's nice to have it there as an option. We can also ask about the general mood. *"How are you feeling? What's it like for you to be in this space?"*

As we ask these questions, even if the client doesn't respond, if they don't respond outwardly, the questions tend to evoke a richer textured inner experience of what's happening. But most often, the client will reply and tell us.

*"Oh, I can see such and such. I can hear that or something else."* and, as they say it themselves, that adds to the richness, it adds to the texture, it adds to the experience. It makes it more real, more memorable, more accessible.

So this process of inviting someone into hypnosis, by simply inviting them to re-experience and imagine something that they like to do, to invite focus, to invite absorption and then for us to comment on the changes and ask for enhanced texture around these changes can be such a simple, such an easy, such an elegant, such a respectful way for any individual to find their own individual way into their own individual hypnotic experience, in contrast to a more rigid way of suggesting that someone do this, that or the other, according to our ideas, as a function of our expertise and professional knowledge.

## FINDING WHAT'S MISSING

Before we invited someone into hypnosis, we have already clarified with them what was missing for them, what it was that they were wanting, what they would be wanting to look for. And now we've invited a client into a focused, absorbed experience, experiencing something that they like, and we know that when someone's doing something they like, they are very resourceful. So we can next simply invite a client, focused and absorbed in their experience, to look around and find whatever it is that is missing for them, to find whatever it is that they're looking for, to find whatever it is that they want that is going to make the difference to them and to their future.

For example, if someone has a problem and we discover that what's missing for them is confidence, and if what they like doing is horse riding, we can assume that, when someone is riding a horse, they won't have any problem with confidence, not if they like it. They will have learnt about that. So we can invite someone to go for a ride, get focused, get absorbed and so on, and then, as they're in the experience of riding the horse, to notice how it is to feel confident riding a horse. We can expect, we can anticipate that this will happen. I found that it is always easy for such a client to find what they were looking for.

We're not talking about the problem yet. We're just saying, *"You're on the horse. Notice how it is to feel confident."* That helps the client to connect with the experience of confidence in relation to what they like to do. We can then ask them, as they're riding the horse, as they're experiencing this confidence, to pay attention to their experience of feeling confident and to ask them, as they're spending time with this, as they're getting to know it, as they're becoming familiar with it, to have the experience as if they are actually learning this resource, this experience. So they're actually learning it.

We can say, *"You can soak it up. You can marinade in it. You can sit with it. You can get to know it even better than you already do."* I have found it helpful to spend some time allowing someone to really be with this missing resource. Of course, if it's something that they like, they're not going to complain about it. If someone likes riding a horse, they're not going to complain about having an experience with riding a horse. And if part of that is feeling confident, they're not going to have a problem feeling confident.

We can then have an easy, agreeable, respectful opportunity for a client to have a direct experience within something that they like to do, of precisely what is missing in their problem that, if they had it, they'd be okay.

We've invited someone into an experience that they like. Within this experience that they like, we've invited them to look around and find exactly what it is that they're missing, that they're wanting that would be helpful to them, then help them to connect this resource that they have the experience of in their lives, to connect it with the problem.

That's the next step.

## CONNECTING THE MISSING RESOURCE WITH THE PROBLEM

I have noticed that this connection can happen in very varied ways. Sometimes the connection happens spontaneously before we've even invited it. Sometimes we can make the direct connection ourselves, simply by saying,

*"This is the same as that."* We can ask the client what is it about the experience of doing what you like that could be relevant to the problem so that they can make their own connection. The third way of helping the connection is to speak about learning.

In a workshop years ago, a school teacher told me what she liked to do was, every summer vacation, to go to some part of the world that she'd never been to. She'd just arrive with no plans, no itinerary. She'd just arrive. And what she liked about that was the adventure, the not needing to know, the fun of exploring.

She said she had a problem that she wanted to do something about. She was a school teacher in her early 50s and had reached a stage in her career where she didn't know what she should do. Should she just see her time out until retirement? Should she get further training in special approaches to teaching? Should she go to business school and learn about how to manage so that she could become a school principal? And she said, "I've never been in this situation before."

It was just so delightful to see her face, having said she liked to travel with no plans and have a sense of adventure, to then hear herself say, "I haven't been in this place before and I don't know what to do." And, just in saying that, you could see the cogs turning, the connections happening. She then said, "Okay. I'll be all right now." Her problem was completely resolved. She was delighted. And we didn't really have an opportunity, there was no need for a hypnotic experience. Just looking at what she liked and what was missing in the problem, she was able to make her own connection spontaneously.

Of course, this doesn't happen every time. Sometimes, we need to do something else.

"This is like that"

A young man in his 30s said that he liked riding horses. What he liked about riding horses was the way he felt connected to the horse, as if he and the horse were one. His problem was he was frightened of flying and there was a flight coming up that he felt compelled to take and was terrified. So we had a session in which I invited him to be on his horse, riding his horse, notice how it was to be riding it, to be connected with the horse, to be one with the horse, and to notice how that felt to be at one with the horse.

I then asked him as he was noticing and allowing himself to experience how it was for him to be at one with the horse to sit with that, to soak it up so he could spend some time really connecting with it. And then I said to him, *"This might seem like a rather strange thing for me to say, you might even think it's psychotic, but I'm going to say it anyhow. Riding in a plane is like riding a horse."*

He had this huge smile on his face, looked so relieved, experiencing such a release. He opened his eyes and he said, *"I feel so different now."* I heard subsequently that he had a very nice plane ride, enjoyed it a lot. He felt as if he was so connected with the plane, so connected with the pilot that it was very enjoyable. It wasn't only that it wasn't terrifying as it had been, it became enjoyable.

"How is this like that?"

A third way that we can help someone to make this connection is, instead of us making the connection, as I did with that horse rider and flying, we can ask the client, *"How could you connect them?"*

A woman told me that her favourite way of spending time was cooking. She loved to be in the kitchen, cooking for her family, making up all kinds of different dishes. She liked the fun of it, the creativity of it and the fact that she was nourishing her family. It was very satisfying. The problem was that she was having some difficulty in her work. She was feeling stressed at work, too much pressure. She was wondering whether she was up to it, wondering whether it was too much for her.

So we had an experience of being in her kitchen. Now, I'm no cook, but that doesn't matter. She could cook. So she had a very nice time preparing some dishes and, while she was in the middle of preparing those dishes, while she was in the middle of cooking, knowing that she could taste it and she could add a bit more of this or a bit more of that or, if it wasn't working, she could throw it out and start again. There was absolutely no problem that she had in the kitchen.

So I was then able to ask her, *"What is it about being in the kitchen and cooking that could be helpful for you in your workplace?"* And she looked thoughtful. She was silent for several minutes. And then she said, *"I can turn down the heat. I don't have to put so much chilli in. I can cool it. I can manage it. I can have fun with it. I can create it."* And she then said, *"I'm having some difficulties with my children, but I see now that bringing up my children is like cooking."* She was able to use that connection not only with her work problem, but also with some family issues. All that she needed to do was to see and explore herself how the experience of doing what she liked, the cooking, could contribute to any area of life.

Learning

Often the connection doesn't happen spontaneously. Sometimes the connection doesn't happen when we make it, "This is like that." Sometimes the connection doesn't happen when we ask a client, "How is this like that?" - if we say, "What is it about what you like to do that would be helpful with the problem?" and the client says, "I can't see any way translating that. They're just so different." And it just makes perfect sense that this will be the case sometimes because even if someone can see where they are and they can have a very clear picture, idea, experience of where they want to be, the distance between where they are and where they want to be can be like a huge chasm too big to jump, too big to traverse. So what we need is a bridge.

We can create a bridge with a metaphor of learning. We can say that, "When you first learnt to ride a horse," or we could say, "When you first learnt to cook, you didn't feel confident, you didn't feel connected. It was very difficult. But somehow, as you learnt to ride a horse, somehow as you learnt to cook, you learnt various ways of dealing with that that are now so much a part of you that it's not only not difficult, but you actually enjoy it. And, in the same way that you learnt how to ride a horse, in the same way that you learnt how to cook, in that same way, you could learn how to manage this," whatever 'this' is.

The beautiful thing about bringing learning in is that it translates an experience from a leap of faith into a process, so that it doesn't have to happen instantly, permanently. Rather, like any learning process, it can come and go. You can get it and lose it. You can be certain of it and then forget it. Of course, some things we learn and we've got them permanently, and there are other things that, when we learn them, it's a process. And so, by introducing an experience, the possibility of learning, the pressure is taken off the client, and it is taken off us. I found learning to be a beautiful way of bridging what otherwise might seem an impossible chasm.

## It hasn't happened YET

Sometimes a client still won't make the connection, and instead of feeling discouraged, we can simply invite them to be curious about how, when and where that connection might happen. It might happen tonight while you're eating your meal. It might happen in your dreams or while you're working tomorrow. I might not happen for a week or ten days and you probably won't know when it will happen until afterwards.

We've explored five different ways that can be helpful to connect the missing resource, which we can find in their lives are connected with the problem.

1. It can happen spontaneously
2. We can speak the connection into existence
3. We can invite the client to make the connection
4. We can invite learning
5. It can happen later

There are probably more, but these are five that I have found helpful that I am offering, so you can play with them.

## SPEAKING OF STORIES

Stories are also entrancing by their nature. From childhood we have been spellbound by stories of magic and heroic adventure.

Stories have been part of human culture even before written language. Our ancestors sat around a fire, sharing stories about life, learning, community values. This is how the communities were held together.

At the same time that stories are so crucial to us humans, and as they shape our very being, they are also "just stories." In the presence of a story, we take and leave what we want. We can relate the story to our own individual circumstances, perhaps in a compelling way, but there is nothing forced or imposed. It is this powerful combination of a compelling invitation to relate to the story with an openness to take up the invitation or not that provides such a relevance to the hypnotic experience in particular, and learning and experience in general.

My first meeting with Erickson in 1977 was a three-hour experience where all he did was tell stories. I was enchanted and realised that this approach to therapy had stories at its heart. This left me perplexed because it was clear to me that there were two kinds of people - those that could tell stories and those that couldn't. I was certain that I was in the latter group.

I read books, attended workshops and suffered until I realised that, if I could identify what was missing for a client, any story where this was also missing ... and was found ... would be relevant. It was an epiphany and instead of being in a desert totally devoid of stories, there was a flood, and others have found the same.

For the sake of simplicity, I have found it helpful to think of three kinds of stories: early learning, client stories and life stories.

### Early learning

When we first begin to learn anything new, we have our own individual ways of beginning to make sense of that experience. If there is any initial struggle, it usually falls away and, before long, we find ourselves making good use of the learning, with ease and even pleasure, with no need to be burdened with the memory of any past difficulty we may have had. Milton Erickson used to say that the learning dropped into the unconscious and we could say that it becomes an automatic learning, not requiring that we even recognise that we are using that learning, even though we are.

An Early Learning story is an indirect form of communication in which a client is invited to recall a childhood experience, or acknowledge that such an experience may have occurred, in which a relevant and desired experience has already been learnt. It can be useful in a general sense to seed the idea of learning itself, and so help to set up the mood of learning in the hypnotic experience.

Even if a client can't recall the memory of learning to walk, if they walked into the session, they are demonstrating that this skill has been learnt by them, and if they can't recall its learning, then there is a strong implication that there are many other skills that have been learnt without the need to recall the experience of learning them either.

It can be helpful, in choosing an early learning story, to ask about the client's likes. If they like walking, then it will be safe to speak about learning to walk. If they like swimming, then learning to swim will be relevant. Asking about likes avoids the pitfall of talking about learning to do something which has not been learnt, or which may be associated with a trauma. Mentioning learning to swim to someone who almost drowned will be unhelpful, and learning to ride a bike won't connect with anyone who never learnt that skill.

*If a client wanted to overcome anxiety in a performance, they might distinguish the missing experience as confidence in the presence of a potentially critical audience. If the client tells us they like reading, we can safely and usefully speak about the experience of learning letters and numbers. So we might say "When you wanted to learn to write your name, you had to get used to making some mistakes and correcting them. When a stranger came into the room, it may have felt impossible to write your name even though you had just written it by yourself. It didn't take long before you were feeling very confident about your ability to write your name, no matter who was there, no matter where you were, no matter what the circumstances, because you realised that that ability was within you, and had nothing to do with anything outside yourself. It felt so good to discover that and can feel good now to use that discovery in any way you need to or want to."*

*If a client wanted to go to the supermarket without panicking, they might identify the missing experience as a sense of security in previously distressful circumstances. If they enjoy going for walks in the country, we can safely and usefully speak about walking as a relevant skill, which has already been learnt. We might say "When you first learnt to walk, you probably did some falling over. Falling over is an important part of learning to walk for any individual. How did you get past that falling? How did you get past the fear of falling? Did you just forget about it? Did you persist until it became easier? Then you were able to feel secure within yourself, knowing even if you did fall occasionally, you could cope with that, you could handle that with a sense of achievement and accomplishment because everyone has their own ways of overcoming difficulties."*

The use of an early learning story is yet another way that we can work respectfully and coherently with clients, to speak to their competences, since they have already learnt many skills, and evoke the mood of expectancy which can be so delightful as a way of generating change that is fitting and relevant to the individual client.

## Client stories

These have the form of "I had a client not unlike yourself who ... [describe client's problem] ... and [describe solution]."

This helps the client to feel less weird - "I'm not the only one" - and also creates the possibility of a resolution. "If they found a solution, maybe I can also."

## Life stories

These are stories where the resource that is missing is found, but instead of relating to another client, they relate to a broader sphere - nature, mythology, a film or book - being even more indirect than a clinical story.

*Scientists wanted to use a supercomputer to find the meaning of existence. They gathered data from every possible source – historical, biological, anthropological – having explored every possible avenue. They fed in all this accumulated data, taking many days and nights, sometimes wondering if their task would ever be finished. Finally, when the last bite of information was entered, they set the computations going and left the mega machine to do its work. After what seemed like an eternity, the computer completed its superhuman task and printed out the answer to the problem that had been alluding philosophers from the earliest times. The words appeared on the printout – "That reminds me of a story."*

Stories are an ancient and deep part of humanity. Human beings are deeply embedded in stories and archaic explanations of our place in life and what it all means to humans to be human. Our individual and social identities are constructed and perpetuated in the stories we tell about ourselves and live individually and socially. We are our stories and our stories are us. They give meaning and purpose to our lives.

## Choices

*"A Native American grandfather tells his young grandson that he has two wolves inside of him, struggling with each other. The first is the wolf of peace, love and kindness. The other wolf is fear, greed and hatred. "Which wolf will win, Grandfather?" asks the young boy. "Whichever one you feed," is the reply."*

This is very different from simply saying that we have a choice about our future. The message is there, but when we listen to the story, we make our own conclusion and don't feel instructed or preached to about what we should do.

## Monsters

*A long time ago, before humans walked on the earth, all the animals lived in harmony with one exception. Nose Monster was* causing increasing fear because he would walk up to an animal and stick his hard spiky proboscis into their soft underbelly and suck out all their blood, leaving a shriveled up bag of skin.

Desperate to find a way of protecting themselves from this monster, the other animals called a meeting and coyote was elected to take charge because he was so cunning and clever. Coyote ordered the animals to go into the forest and bring back garlands of prickly bushes and spiky branches. He ordered other animals to cook up two huge vats of blood soup, which he placed, steaming hot in the meeting hut. He organised the animals to decorate the doorway with the garlands of prickles and the spiky branches, and then went looking for Nose Monster.

Before long coyote found Nose Monster, who was looking wide eyed with hunger and wanted to get close to coyote. Coyote told him about the two huge vats of blood soup and offered to escort Nose Monster to the hut. Nose monster was very keen.

In the hut, Nose Monster rushed up to the first vat of steaming blood soup and greedily stuck his spiky proboscis into it, noisily sucked it dry. He looked pleased, and was beginning to feel full, but the other vat was too tempting so he stuck his proboscis into that vat and noisily sucked up every last drop of blood soup. He was so full he could hardly move. He was so bloated, that he could hardly stand. But he was Nose Monster and so, greedy for blood as ever, he turned towards Coyote. "Now it's your turn," he said, lunging clumsily at Coyote who deftly stepped aside so that Nose Monster rolled onto his round, bloated stomach. He *struggled to get to his feet and lunged at Coyote again, and again Coyote easily stepped aside. Each time Nose Monster lunged, Coyote moved closer and closer to the doorway of the meeting hut until, just as Coyote stepped into the doorway, and Nose Monster feared that his next blood meal might get away, he made a super huge attempt to get Coyote. And his body, hugely bloated with all the blood soup, fell onto the prickles and spikes lining the doorway, and exploded into a million pieces.*

*And that is how the mosquito came into existence.*

Is this story about overcoming fear, dealing with problems before they become large, starting small with any endeavour, finding the right strategy, working together, being realistic, giving up greed, lightening up? It might be about any of these, or a combination, or something totally different. The story is a story, and each individual has the opportunity to remind themselves of anything that is relevant to their individual situation. The speaker might even find out what the story was about after the listener responds.

Creating Possibilities - Indirectly

An adolescent may have been inspired by Superman, Mighty Mouse, or Grace Kelly.

An adult might be moved by modern heroes, like Nelson Mandela, Mahatma Gandhi, Stoltenberg, or ancient heroes, like the Buddha, Moses, Jesus, Mohammad, Lao Tzu.

Reading stories about these people create the possibility for a listener. Something that may have seemed impossible becomes possible. "If they did it, it must be possible. Perhaps I can do it also." When we hear the stories of these people, we may change the direction of our own lives. When Mandela spoke of the importance to him of his small patch of garden in prison, anyone listening may spend more time in their garden and feel more gratitude as well.

Leaders are strong leaders by creating strong stories to make sense to their followers. Unfortunately, not all stories are helpful and some of the worst atrocities have happened from atrocious stories about ethnic differences, whether they claim superiority or inferiority.

## The Experts - A Sufi Tale

*A man thought to be dead was taken by his friends for burial. When the coffin was about to be lowered into the grave, the man suddenly came to life and began to bang on the lid of the coffin.*

*The coffin was opened; the man sat up. "What are you doing?" he said to the assembled crowd. "I am alive. I am not dead."*

*His words were met with stunned silence. Finally, one of the mourners said, "Friend, both the doctors and the priests have certified that you are dead. The experts can hardly be wrong."*

*So the lid was screwed on again and he was duly buried.*

## Wisdom?

*An American investment banker was at the pier of a small coastal Mexican village when a small boat with just one fisherman docked. Inside the small boat were several large yellow fin tuna. The American complimented the Mexican on the quality of his fish and asked how long it took to catch them.*

*The Mexican replied, "Only a little while." The American then asked why didn't he stay out longer and catch more fish?*

*The Mexican said he had enough to support his family's immediate needs. The American then asked, "But what do you do with the rest of your time?"*

*The Mexican fisherman said, "I sleep late, fish a little, play with my children, take siesta with my wife, Maria, stroll into the village each evening where I sip wine and play guitar with my amigos. I have a full and busy life."*

*The American scoffed, "I am a Harvard MBA and could help you. You should spend more time fishing and with the proceeds, buy a bigger boat. With the proceeds from the bigger boat, you could buy several boats. Eventually, you would have a fleet of fishing boats. Instead of selling your catch to a middleman, you would sell directly to the processor, eventually opening your own cannery. You would control the product, processing and distribution. You would need to leave this small coastal fishing village and move to Mexico City, then LA and eventually NYC where you will run your expanding enterprise."*

*The Mexican fisherman asked, "But, how long will this all take?" To which the American replied, "Fifteen to 20 years."*

*"But what then?"*

*The American laughed and said that's the best part. "When the time is right, you would announce an IPO and sell your company stock to the public and become very rich, you would make millions."*

*"Millions... Then what?"*

*The American said, "Then you would retire. Move to a small coastal fishing village where you would sleep late, fish a little, play with your kids, take siesta with your wife, stroll to the village in the evenings where you could sip wine and play your guitar with your amigos."*

## COMPLETING THE HYPNOSIS SESSION

When the session is complete, all we need to do is to allow the client to shift their focus so that, instead of being focused on their likes and their connections, they can have a more usual way of focusing in the present time.

We don't have to have some kind of formal way of bringing someone out of hypnosis, like techniques that I learnt when I first learnt hypnosis, counting from 10 down to one, asking someone to walk up some steps and so on. But when we think of hypnosis as an experience that involves focus and absorption as an extension of the common everyday trance, then there's no need for any such formal proceedings.

When someone's reading a book and they get to the end of the book, they don't need to do anything specific; or the end of a chapter, they don't need to do anything specific to complete that. They just put the book down and then do whatever they need to do. They get up from the chair, move around and do whatever they need to do. I found that when we finished the hypnotic session, all we need to do is to invite someone, when they're ready to do what they need to do, to complete their experience.

There is still a strange mood around hypnosis. And I really love what Erickson told me about a situation that happened some years ago. It was at a conference and a woman had volunteered to be a hypnotic subject. After the demonstration was finished, the therapist instructed her to come out of hypnosis and she wasn't budging! They tried all kinds of things, counting, coming up stairs, giving indirect suggestions and so on. Nothing was happening and, after two hours, they started to get worried.

Erickson was in the conference and we know that Erickson was always the go-to person whenever there was a problem. Erickson went up to this woman sitting in the chair in her own experience, sitting on the stage, and he leant over and made a couple of comments gently into her ear and then left. After about a minute or two, she suddenly opened her eyes, got off that chair and hurriedly left the stage.

The people organising the conference were curious about what had happened and cornered Erickson and asked him, "What did you do? Did you give her a double bind? Did you give her an indirect suggestion? What was it that you did?"

Erickson said, "I didn't do anything complicated. I just told her that, although she hadn't had anything to drink for three hours, her kidneys were working and drip, drip, drip, slowly her bladder was filling up and, if she didn't get off that chair soon, she might end up wetting her pants."

What I love about that story is that it demystifies the kind of weird thing about hypnosis as if it's a general anaesthetic.

I had a couple of personal examples myself. There was one woman, who was seeing me for a particular problem. I don't even remember what it was now. It was a long time ago. And she complained about my fee and said that it was outrageously high. I agreed with her and said that I wouldn't pay that amount, but in any case, she'd agreed, so that was the situation. The hypnosis happened and, at the end of the hour, she was not budging. There was someone else waiting in the waiting room and, because I knew she had a sensitivity about finances, I said to her, "Take all the time you need coming out of trance, but just be aware that the meter is ticking." She opened her eyes very promptly.

A man, who was very shy in the presence of women, at the end of the session, again, was reluctant to come out of hypnosis. I told him there was no need for him to hurry, but that there was a woman in the waiting room, who was my next client, and she would be coming in, in a moment. As long as he didn't mind a strange woman sitting on his knee, he could stay there as long as he wanted. He opened his eyes very quickly.

After Erickson, I think of someone coming out of hypnosis as being a very natural process. If someone is having some trouble in their life and we do some hypnotic work so that they're feeling better, it makes perfect sense to me that they might be reluctant to come out of the comfort that they experience in hypnosis into the relative discomfort of the reality.

I hope these comments are somewhat helpful in demystifying the process of coming out of hypnosis in the same way that, when we think of hypnosis as an experience of focused absorption, as an extension of the common everyday trance, the process of inviting someone into hypnosis is also nothing special.

## AFTER HYPNOSIS

What's different?

Completing the session

When someone comes out of trance, we want to check with them to see what benefit they have had from the session and so it can be very helpful to ask a client, "What's different now, compared with how you felt before we started?" This is a different question from, "Was that helpful?" because, if we say, "Was that helpful?" then the client in a position of having to decide if it was helpful or not, whereas when we say, "What's different now?" there is an assumption that something's different and then the client goes looking for those differences.

Anything that the client says is different is something that we can explore with them to validate, congratulate them, to consolidate that and perhaps even invite them, after they leave the session, to be open to noticing how they can have more of that. If someone says, "I feel more confident than I did before," or "I feel more comfortable than I did before," or "I'm clearer than I was before we started the session," then we can invite this client to be aware and notice anytime they're feeling confident, comfortable or clear. This helps to connect the hypnotic experience that happened in our presence to connect it with their life, which is of course, where they live.

If we ask someone, "What's different?" some people will, of course, say, "Nothing's different." And it's so important to know that nothing is different. We can explore with them what was missing for them that would have made a difference and helps to clarify the direction, the focus for the next session. Rather than us assuming we've done a good job, everything's fine, if we ask the client, this gives us a way of refining, clarifying and consolidating any benefits and anything that will then need to be done differently in subsequent sessions.

One of the useful invitations I found for people is to remove the pressure by saying something like, *"Don't go too far with this. Don't go too fast with this. Take your time with this. You've had that problem for all that time so it's only sensible, it's only to be expected that you're allowed to take some time to let that learning settle. So please be gentle with yourself and allow the changes to happen in their own time, in their own way, at their own pace."* I found it to be very useful to Invite someone to have that attitude to their change and it also takes the pressure off us.

Finally, at the very end of the session, say, "Thank you." There's something about the phrase 'thank you' that has a wonderful way of creating a completion. 'Thank you' can even be thought of as a declaration of completion. I've noticed that sometimes a client will say, "Thank you," before I'm necessarily ready to stop, letting me know that they're ready to stop.

'Thank you' then is a wonderful phrase that adds value to everything. If we say to a client, "Thank you for trusting me to be part of your resolution, thank you for trusting me for being part of your solving this problem that has been so troublesome to you," it is a beautiful way to finish a session. And I invite you to try that and see what your experience is.

## GETTING UNSTUCK

### The Comfort Of Validation

If someone goes into a supermarket and they don't know what they went there to buy, they can be there a long time and end up getting frustrated with the outcome. If the same person goes into the same supermarket and they know they want bread and milk, they may have to ask for help to find them, but there would be no problem. They will get what they went for.

In the process of supervising people over the years, the questions that always helps to clarify stuckness for a therapist, when they're working with a client, the questions that I found so helpful are the basic questions that we are exploring: what does this client like to do and what's missing for this client?

When we ask, "What does this client like to do?" that tells us where to look for the resource of someone that is stuck because they've become disconnected from it. Asking, "What's missing for this client," helps to focus our attention on this client and what it is that we're looking for. So then we have a winning combination of knowing what we're looking for and knowing where to look for it. Clients get stuck when they don't know what's missing. And therapists get stuck if they don't know what's missing for their client or for themselves. So we can all get stuck if we don't know where to look or what is missing.

There's a wonderful Sufi story about Mulla Nasreddin. He was down on his hands and knees under a streetlight, obviously looking for something. And his long-suffering, well-intended neighbour comes along and says, "What are you doing?" Nasreddin said, "I'm looking for my house keys." So the neighbour joins Nasreddin on his knees, looking for the house key. After a while, they're not finding the key and the neighbour says to Nasreddin, "Are you sure you dropped the keys here?" to which Nasreddin replied, "Oh, no. I dropped it over there." The puzzled neighbour says, "If you dropped the keys over there, how come we're looking here?" to which Nasreddin replied, "Well, the light's better here."

A friend told me of two tourists, who were lost in Ireland. They went into a local pub, put a map on the bar and told the publican that they were lost. The publican scratched his head and, after some time, perusing the map said, "Well, I wouldn't be starting from here." The Irish have a wonderful way of revealing some of the absurdity of our human condition.

A man had been in a psychiatric hospital for a long time and all he would say was, "I shouldn't be here." Erickson replied, "But you are here." And when this eventually clicked with the man, he said, "Oh, my goodness! What do I need to do to get out of here?" He needed to get to where he was before he could move on.

Many clients can only begin to resolve their stuckness after their suffering has been significantly acknowledged. We can help by saying sincerely to such a client, "You've been through hell. This has been terrible for you. You've suffered so much and nothing seems to have helped. I can imagine that you must feel desperate at times." These kind of statements can be like water in the desert. They are affirming of the client's legitimacy in their experience.

I've also noticed, when I've offered these comments to a client, they have often been so relieved. It's brought tears to their eyes at times. When they experience the relief that, at last, someone recognises the intensity and the legitimacy of their suffering instead of rushing in to assist to relieve them. It's so tempting for us therapists to want to lessen the client's suffering so that we don't feel bad.

Validating a client's suffering, letting them know that we see that their suffering is legitimate, can be a wonderful first step towards finding what's missing and getting some movement where there had previously been only stuckness.

## THE RELIEF OF INCORPORATION

Hypnosis used to be thought of as a rather delicate state, something to be protected, and so should happen in a quiet, climate-controlled environment, with soft lighting and peaceful music playing in the background. We now see that hypnosis is not like an anaesthetic, and more like an experience of focused attention, familiar to all of us in our everyday life. And so we can look to see how we can facilitate attentiveness and absorption rather than avoiding any minute potential distraction.

While some find focusing on reading, learning, etc., easier in a silent environment, others don't mind or even prefer some background activity, doing homework better while watching TV. Also the quieter the environment, the louder any noise seems, so it can be useful to have everyday experiences including potential disruptions and noises be part of the hypnotic experiences. If someone comes in from a hot day into an air-conditioned office, enjoys the coolness and has to return to the heat, how long does the coolness last. My preference is to connect the hypnotic experience to everyday life as much as possible, and for most of us, this includes noise, concerns and a multitude of potential distractions.

Incorporation is a wonderful expression of the principles in the Ericksonian approach – accept what the client brings and use it – and extends the acceptance and utilisation to include potential external distractions, client and therapist concerns.

It is a process that can achieve an acceptance and inclusion of external sounds, and concerns of the client and therapist. Instead of being disruptive, they can become part of the hypnotic experience. When more potential disruptions are included as legitimate components of the hypnotic session, the experience becomes fuller and rounder, making the translation and transportation of the experience with us into their own living smoother and more real. This can keep the therapist alert, and so add to their attentiveness and delight.

Incorporating externals:

We can offer a direct suggestion that the louder the external sound becomes, the more absorbed the client can be in their experience of hypnosis. This can be helpful when we know something is disturbing, but risks introducing a disturbance by bringing a client's attention to it when they may not have noticed it. We can be more indirect and playful by alluding to an experience [phone ringing, plane overhead] with comments such as "This experience can ring true to you," "Your learning can go to a higher plain [plane]."

Incorporating client concerns:

Clients have concerns which can distract them from their experience. They might be thinking "Am I doing the right thing?" or "How should I be behaving?" or "Is this hypnosis?" We can reassure individuals if these concerns are expressed or we can pre-empt them by suggesting "Feel free to do what you need to do at any time, recognising that you will at any moment be doing exactly what you need to do to achieve what is useful to you." or "Hypnosis is different for different individuals. It's more important for you to have the experience you are having so you can learn what you need to learn, so you can be unconcerned."

Should a client be concerned that they don't understand, we can say, "Your understandings are yours and you can reach them in your own time, at your own pace, in any way that feels right to you."

If a client has some fear of losing control, we can offer "I'm talking, but this is your experience and you can respond in any way that is helpful to you. I can suggest that you close your eyes, but you can let your eyes close when you are ready."

If someone is worried they might not remember the content of the session and so lose any benefit, we can suggest "You can be unconcerned knowing that you will only recall what is relevant to you and your learning."

Concerns about going deeply enough can be addressed with "You won't go any deeper than you need to."

Incorporating therapist's concerns:

As therapists, we find ourselves getting stuck, having doubts, feeling uncertain. We could just suffer, stutter, and hope; we could say, "I'm stuck," or "I'm uncertain," etc., and while this may provide some personal respite, it is hardly helpful to the client. It can, however, be extremely helpful if we express our concern, externalise it, but in a way that can aid the process rather than hinder it.

If we are thinking "What do I say next?" we can say, "I don't need to talk all the time."

If we are stuck on what to do next, we can offer "What I do is much less important than the way you can use this experience for your own benefit and betterment."

If we feel uncertain about how we are doing, articulating, "You don't need to attend to me except [accept] in ways that can be useful to you," or "This is your experience, not mine; is happening for you, not for me; so you can look forward to discovering how you can make your own good use of this experience" can be a relief to us AND benefit the client.

Incorporation can take care of our shared mood, so a potential block is averted, doubts are averted, and the hypnotic process can proceed towards the client's goal with mutual satisfaction.

# SECTION 3
## EXPERIENCING HYPNOSIS

### An Introduction

When I first learned about hypnosis from a traditional, formal approach, I was fascinated and, at the same time, overwhelmed by what was called hypnotic phenomena. These hypnotic phenomena, like the word 'phenomena' itself from the Greek, were very complex, very technical. I'd learnt about them and they seemed so strange. They were called 'association, dissociation, time distortion, age regression, age progression, amnesia, anaesthesia, analgesia,' a long list of highly technical words that only served to intimidate me and other people learning at the same time as me. I didn't find this helpful for my process of learning.

When Erickson spoke about the common everyday trance and invited us to approach hypnosis as an extension of the common everyday trance, this resulted in a shift in our appreciation of hypnosis from something that was weird, alien, highly technical, requiring expert management and only useful to a few who were hypnotisable to the way any person can become focused and absorbed in many experiences, particularly experiences that they like to do.

In the same spirit as bringing hypnosis out of the ivory tower of weirdness and academia and bringing it to ground, bringing it to everyday life, so, in the same way, we can look at the various hypnotic phenomena as extensions of common everyday experiences that we all have had at various times in many different situations. We have all found at times that we can be really connected with these experiences.

We can all focus on something, get absorbed in it and become connected to that. Listening to music, reading a book, walking in nature, we can really feel that connection. And, at the same time as we might be listening to music, for example, we become disconnected from an awareness of our feet or the gas bill or what happened during the day or what might happen tomorrow. So, in our everyday experience, there is a continual interplay between what we connect with or associate with and what we disconnect from or dissociate from. It's a common, everyday experience; nothing weird, nothing complicated.

We all know, if we go on a holiday, the time can pass so quickly. Doing something boring, time can go so slowly. We've all had that experience. So we don't have to make it into something more complex, like calling it 'time distortion,' as if that's some prerogative of a select few. It's something we've all had a lot of experience of.

We can all look at a school photograph and remember the teacher that we had in fourth grade or we can look at a memento, look at a souvenir from a holiday last year, 20 years ago. When we look at those photos, when we look at that souvenir, we can't help but remember some part of the experience that we had. And so that capacity to remember something that happened in the past can be the beginning of a focused, absorbed experience that will help to connect us with our past. I find that much more helpful to think of that experience rather than something complex like 'age regression.'

We can look forward to a holiday, look at a brochure, look forward to the birth of a child. We can look forward to something and anticipate it. Children look forward to Father Christmas or the Tooth Fairy or the Easter Bunny. We can all anticipate something. And if we take an ordinary, everyday experience of anticipation and then focus on that and become absorbed in it, we can create a hypnotic experience. We can do that as an extension of ordinary, everyday happenings. We don't have to talk about age progression.

Am I the only person who has had an experience of coming into a room and thinking, "Now, what did I come in here for?" or "Where did I park my car?" or "What was on the shopping list that I forgot to bring with me?" We can all forget things. Forgetting is part of everyday life. And so, if we begin with the notion of forgetting, as an ordinary human experience, we don't have to be involved with something technical or weird, like 'amnesia.'

In dealing with pain, there are two aspects that are troublesome to us. One is the sensation and the other is how bothered we are by it. And, in medical terms, producing some numbness so that we don't feel the sensations is called 'anaesthesia,' not feeling. And when something is there, but not bothering us, the medical technical term is 'analgesia.' But instead of getting involved with these technicalities, we can very easily notice that, in the course of our everyday experience, there are a lot of sensations that we already don't notice: feet on the floor, someone wearing glasses. We don't notice those.

People living near an airport don't hear the aeroplanes. People living on a busy road don't hear the traffic. The sounds are there, the sensations are potentially there, but somehow, they're not noticed.

Also, we've all had many, many experiences of having sensations and not being bothered by them. Sometimes a child can make a noise, or cry and we can think, "Oh, aren't they cute? Isn't that wonderful that they're letting us know that they're hungry and need their nappy changed?" There are other sensations that can be so comforting, not only not bothered by them, but actually enjoyable.

This way of appreciating allows us, and our clients, to have a natural and easy access to these experiences instead of being overwhelmed and anxious about what I was originally taught as advanced "techniques."

This long list of potentially complex, convoluted, specialised areas of learning can be linked with everyday experiences and so they become more available for clients to make use of and they become more available for us, as therapists, to foster, to encourage, to amplify instead of having to learn some very complex, convoluted series of techniques.

## CONNECTING AND DISCONNECTING

Anyone can focus and become absorbed in some everyday activity, such as reading a book, watching a movie … and in that experience it's not uncommon for some alteration of perception to happen. We can become so connected with the reading or watching that we become disconnected from our surroundings.

Every aspect of hypnosis is simply a function of connecting with some experiences and then disconnecting from others. The very first time I met Milton Erickson, he asked me what I wanted to learn and I told him what I'd learnt so far about the use of hypnosis for pain management didn't really make sense to me.

He just nodded to me and had me sit on a small stool and I sat there, really intensely focusing on his words. I'd travelled halfway around the world. He was not easy to understand because, as a result of his polio, he was not able to wear false teeth, his tongue wasn't working properly and he had quite strong southern accent. So, all in all, it took an effort just to understand what he was saying.

He continued to tell stories, stories about an artist, about a sculptor, about a lawyer, story after story. And, as I began to connect, to focus, to get absorbed in his stories, I became disconnected from my surroundings, from the room, from my feet although I did stay connected with an increasing discomfort in my knees, as my elbows pushed into my knees, leaning forward, straining to understand his words.

And as he continued to tell stories for the next three hours, I learned a lot about connecting, about disconnecting as an experience although I was unable to put my experience into clear words. At the end of that time, I said to him that I wasn't quite sure what he was getting to in all of those stories. He had given me the three-hour version. Then he gave me the ultra-short version by saying, "What we experience depends on how we direct our attention."

He was giving me a description of the way, when we direct our attention in different directions, we create different experiences. And also how we direct our attention. Do we do this effortfully, do we do this as a way of avoiding something or can we be curious about it? Different ways to direct our attention.

When we invite someone into hypnosis, we might ask them what they like to do and then, as a way of creating an individual hypnotic experience for each person, we can invite them to start to focus on some part of that experience and become absorbed in that. If someone were to like walking in nature and we invited them into such an experience, then the more they begin to connect with the hypnotic experience of walking in nature, the more disconnected they become from the room in which we are both sitting.

And in a more ordinary way, a person can be sitting, reading a book and if the book becomes sufficiently interesting, the reader begins to connect with the experience in the book and they forget about their feet, they forget about what they had for lunch. They disconnect from so many things as they connect with the experience that's happening in the reading. If the phone should ring, then the reader will disconnect from the book and connect with the phone. There's nothing special about this. It's just a part of what we humans do.

A person could speak to someone on the phone and have a very connected conversation with them, hang up the phone and then, not only are they disconnected from the person that they were speaking with on the phone, they actually become disconnected from the phone itself and start to reconnect with the book. And, if we look at our experience, we could see that we are continually in a flux of connecting with this and disconnecting with that and then connecting with something else and disconnecting from what we were connecting with previously. It's just how we function in our life. Nothing special.

Once we see that this capacity to connect and disconnect is something that's available to us, to each of us in our own unique ways, then this becomes yet one more resource that we can bring to any situation and help to resolve it.

## ELASTIC TIME

In the Greek language, there are two words for time. One is chronos, which I understand translates into clock time, and the other is kairos, which can be translated into timely or, as the Japanese car manufacturers like to say, "Just in time."

Now, chronos, clock time, is a relatively new experience for us humans. It only became a popular part of our everyday life after the industrial revolution, where it became important to have factory workers assemble at a particular time, to coordinate their activities. On the other hand, kairos, or timely, has been described as when someone's in a slip lane, waiting to go onto a motorway, finds a way in which the car can enter the traffic on the motorway; not after a certain time, but somehow in a timely fashion.

And, of course, while such a person is waiting to get onto the motorway, if they're in a hurry, it can feel like they're waiting for a very long time while if it happens easily, they might say, "Well, that was timely." But in the same way, it's as if time is not a function. Time is not something that we pay attention to. It's more like timeless or out of time because it's timely. It just happens.

My wife likes to quote Douglas Adams in the Hitchhiker's Guide To The Galaxy in saying that "Time is an illusion. Lunchtime doubly so." And in the quirky humour of that man, of that author, we can imagine that someone in a workplace where they were bored, that the time leading up to lunchtime might seem to really drag and, knowing that after the end of lunchtime, there's more boring work to do that lunch hour could go very quickly.

We've all had an experience like looking forward to a holiday and the closer the holiday gets, the slower the clock seems to move. It's as if it will never happen, just like a little kid waiting for Christmas or a birthday. It seems to take forever. Then we get on to the holiday and we arrive, we blink our eyes three or four times and it's already time to go home. A kid waiting for a birthday party, first the party starts, a moment later, it's time for everybody to go home. It seemed so short.

So we know, from our own everyday experience how our measurement of time by a clock and our experience of time, as an experience, vary tremendously. And there is that expression 'time flies when you're having fun.' It's a cliché, which just reveals the obviousness of something that we know. And if time can fly when we're having fun that alerts us to the fact that we know how to have time fly. So in that way, someone can have time fly when they're having pain, when they're having discomfort or where they're having something they don't want. If it can fly, it can fly.

This experience that happens in our everyday life can be something that we can use clinically. When someone in a hypnotic experience becomes very focused and very absorbed, half an hour can go past, an hour can go past and it's not uncommon for a client to be surprised at just how much time has passed. It's not uncommon for someone, after an hour, to feel that the experience only lasted five or 10 minutes. So the way time can expand and contract is part of our everyday life and like many experiences, it can be highlighted and explored with greater intensity in hypnosis. It also then becomes a resource to use in our clinical work.

## TIME TRAVEL

We can look at a school photo and have pleasant or unpleasant memories about people in that class, in Grade 4, the teacher that we liked or couldn't stand in Grade six. We can look at the photograph and, looking at the photograph, we can remember some of what happened.

If we were to take that experience of looking at the photograph, which is a very familiar, a very everyday experience, we could start to focus on some part of that, one, or the other people in the photograph, the classroom, furniture, the picture on the wall, whatever it might be that we start to focus on, and get absorbed in that. The experience of becoming focused and absorbed in the memory has the effect of allowing us to have the experience as if we are increasingly in that experience, as it was then.

We can have a souvenir of a holiday that we went on as a child, or a couple of weeks ago. We can look at that souvenir, glance at it and have a fleeting memory, "Ah, yes. We were there. That's what that was." And if we were to look at that souvenir and start to focus on it, start to get absorbed in where we bought it, where we found it, and allow some more texture to happen around the experience, then we have the ingredients for a hypnotic experience, which is as if we are increasingly at that place, at that time where we found that souvenir.

There's nothing really remarkable about this. Its just part of our everyday life and, like any experience in our everyday life, there can be an accentuation, an enhancement of these everyday experiences, so they become more intense that we can call hypnosis. They become even more real and instead of a fleeting recollection, we can be and have an experience of being in that place at that time.

So, if the client comes with some problem that is a result of something that happened in the past, we can have the opportunity to engage with the experience that that client has, not to go back and find out what actually happened, because memory is not like that, but to have the experience of returning to a time before the problem happened and having this client remember or imagine an experience before that problem happened so that they can then gather up some resources, gather up some preparedness to deal with that situation.

We can also, because memories are created, play with some of those memories, mess with them and alter them. *A woman told me she was getting married and was concerned because all of her previous long-term relationships had been disastrous. And the reason they were disastrous, she said, was because she was brought up in a conflictual family. Her mother and father fought recurrently and quite violently. She said, "I learnt that from them." I want to emphasise that that was her interpretation, not mine.*

*So we played hypnotically with some of those memories. She remembered a time when her parents were arguing in the kitchen and she was cowering under the kitchen table, terrified. I asked her what she would prefer. She said, "I'd rather they stopped fighting and gave me a hug." So, reminding her that we were just imagining this, she could imagine that they could stop fighting and they could give her a hug. She could do that. And she enjoyed the experience. She remembered another incident. Her father was driving, her mother in the front passenger seat and she was in the back. More arguments. And when I asked her what she would prefer, she said, "I would like an ice cream." She even decided on what flavour she would like. So she was able to imagine that her parents stopped fighting and bought her an ice cream.*

*After we had played with a number of memories like this, at the end of the hypnotic experience, she looked very peaceful and said, "I know I just imagined those pleasant memories, but now I'm starting to realise that there were some good times. It wasn't all bad." And she was wistful as she said that. I didn't see her after that. I don't know whether her marriage went well, but it was very clear to me and to her that she left with a very different future than she came in with.*

And so, when someone has some problem that somehow they feel tethered to some past event, there are ways that we can influence their experience of their part that can be helpful to them.

We can plan a holiday; we can plan a celebration, a family gathering, something in the future. We can look forward to it. We can anticipate it. It's ordinary for us to be able to anticipate something and to look forward to it. Because hypnosis is a way of accentuating and intensifying these common everyday experiences, we can help someone to imagine some future occurrence, become absorbed in it after focusing on it and have the experience increasingly as if that is what is happening, even though they know intellectually it hasn't happened yet. They can have the experience as if some preferred future is happening in the present.

A woman told me that she wanted to lose weight and didn't see how that was possible. She said, "I've always been overweight. I was a fat baby, a chubby child and I've been overweight all of my life." So in hypnosis, she really enjoyed imagining going into her future and being the weight that she wanted, being the weight that she preferred. And by allowing her to have the experience in an unhurried, timely way, she was able to have the experience as if she had already lost the weight.

Tongue in cheek and with a straight face, I said to her, "You don't need to wait until you've lost the weight to have the experience as if you've already achieved what you wanted." As a result of this, instead of her dieting with a resignation and the hopelessness of knowing it was only temporary, she was able to imagine and look forward to that result. This allowed her to shed the excess weight, taking her own time without any effort in a way that felt really good for her. So, when someone tells us they don't see the possibility of something happening in the future, some time travel into the future can make all the difference.

Steve de Shazer's Miracle Question is simply a shorthand version of this.

Helping someone to experience a preferred future is a skill for us to have. It can be so helpful as an extension of the kind of experience that we're all familiar with, without having to resort to some highly technical jargon, but rather just engaging normally in an everyday fashion with someone so that they can then achieve what they want in their way.

Revisiting the past can be useful when there is a sense of incompletion or dissatisfaction so we can play with the memory and alter it to something preferable.

Imagining the future is going to be useful when someone feels stuck and blocked about the possibility of a change, so they can then have an experience of a preferred outcome.

*When I was in general medical practice, the last 10 deliveries I was part of were hypnotic deliveries. Nine of the mothers were having their first baby, and none of them needed any medication. The main problem was that the staff were troubled by their quietness and ease. One of the most useful experiences that they reported was the way they could compress the time of their contractions and expand the time between. They also found it helpful to realise that the stronger and more frequent their contractions were, the sooner they could be happily holding their new baby. These simple ideas made such a difference to the mothers … and to their babies.*

## FORGETTING

We've all had the experience of coming into a room, knowing we came into the room for an important reason, and asking ourselves, "What did I come in here for?" We can go to the supermarket and forget the very thing that we went there to get. We buy other things and then somehow we've forgotten what it was that was so important. We can park our car in the car park and forget where we've parked it, or spend a long time looking for our car keys that we've put somewhere.

Forgetting is part of our everyday life. And some of us are better at it than others. I seem to be getting just a little more skilled at forgetting with each passing year. It is not unfamiliar to any of us and, like all of the other hypnotic experiences, we can take something like forgetting as an ordinary, everyday experience and we can co-opt it to be a resource to use, to be of benefit in helping someone to move from some problem that they're suffering from and move towards a solution.

In hypnosis, we can remind someone about the way that we can forget in our everyday experiences. We can meet someone at a party. Two seconds later, we can't remember what their name was. We can even hear something and think, "Ah, now that's something I'll never forget," and even as we're thinking that, the forgetting process has begun.

So when someone is in the experience where they can focus and be open and absorbed in the possibility of forgetting, this can be a wonderful resource when remembering is the problem, like someone with intrusive thoughts, with intrusive voices, with intrusive habits. We can offer the possibility of forgetting, which is what's missing when the memory is overactive and so become part of a solution because there are some things that are best forgotten. We're all more expert at forgetting than we realise.

*I remember a petrol station owner, who wanted to stop smoking. He wanted hypnosis and he said that the problem with the cigarettes for him was that they were always on his mind. Even when he wasn't smoking, the cigarettes were there as a presence. And he said, "I wish I could get them out of my mind."*

*He was very keen to go into hypnosis. It was easy for him. And I offered him the idea of forgetting as something that he could make use of. He seemed quite pleased with the idea. He returned a week later, quite disturbed because he said, "I'm smoking just as much. They're on my mind just as much, but for some reason, I keep forgetting all of the customers' names. It's so embarrassing. People I've known for years, and I can't remember their name."*

*So in hypnosis, I offered the idea that there was a balance between remembering and forgetting and that, as he remembered some things, he could forget others. He'd shown that he had an ability to forget the names of customers so that meant there was at least the possibility of forgetting other experiences, like cigarettes.*

*He called in briefly a week later, saying that he was only having a few cigarettes and he couldn't stand them much longer. Mostly they weren't on his mind at all and the ability to remember his customers' names had returned. He was pleased with the outcome and I was quite delighted and somewhat amused to see the interplay and the flexibility that he demonstrated in relation to remembering and forgetting.*

## NOT NOTICING

Any person can sit on a chair and be comfortable enough and, although there is the possibility of noticing so many sensations that are available to be noticed, it's so easy for us to not notice the sensations of our feet on the floor, our body being supported by the chair, wearing glasses, the sensations of the glasses on the bridge of the nose, behind the ears. People can wear earrings, a watch on their wrist. The sensations of breathing in and out are all potentially noticeable. And yet, it's so easy for us to not notice them.

There can be sounds, external sounds, internal sounds that are potentially audible, but we can acclimatise to those sounds as if they're not there. Sometimes we notice them only when they stop. There is a cliché that a dog can't smell his own smell and so all of our sensations have the potential to be noticed by us, but if we were to be somehow present to all of the physical sensations, all of the sounds, everything that we can see, we would be overwhelmed.

Any person can have the experience of looking for something and not being able to find it, only to discover it's right there, right under their nose. How come they didn't see it? A person wearing glasses is very accustomed to not seeing the glasses, even though, if they were to look with their peripheral vision, they could see the frames, the edge of the lenses and so on.

So this ability that we have to not feel, to not notice sounds, smells, tastes, to not see things are everyday skills in our everyday life. And so they have the potential to be resources that can be used clinically. As with any of these everyday experience, hypnosis has the capacity, to add intensity and texture so that they become more readily available, as an experience.

Erickson said that we have had a lifetime of experience of not noticing sensations.

If someone has pain and we say, "Oh, you don't need to notice that," that's hardly likely to be helpful. But if we begin in a hypnotic experience to remind someone that they don't need to notice the sounds of the traffic outside, they don't need to notice every piece of furniture in the room, they don't need to listen to all of our words, there are so many things that they don't need to notice, this can be a way to gradually ease someone into the experience of not noticing potentially painful sensations.

We've all had the experience of having something that's painful or discomforting, yet we get distracted when something takes our attention and we don't notice the sensations. It's as if they're not there. Someone can have a severe headache. They'd be lying down with the severity of the pain, yet if they were to discover that their house was on fire, they would not be lying there, saying, "The pain is too bad. I can't move." It may even be that, when they're outside of the burning house that they notice that their headache's gone, or perhaps they don't even need to notice it's been gone for some time.

This means that knowing, as we all do from our everyday experience that not noticing various sensory inputs is part of our everyday life can be the beginning, a place to introduce hypnosis so the potential can be extrapolated into some problem area.

*A young woman was only days away from having her first baby. And she was curious about the use of hypnosis in childbirth. And so I was able to sit with her and just remind her that, although she was sitting on the chair, she didn't need to notice the sensation. Although there was a lot of traffic outside, she didn't need to listen to that. Although there were a whole lot of other senses that she could pay attention to, she really didn't need to.*

*Over some 10 minutes, 15 minutes, I was able to introduce her to the idea that she knew more than she realised about not noticing sensations that she didn't need to pay attention to and, as I was talking to her in this way, there were all of the alterations that we've come to recognise as being associated with hypnosis - changes in her breathing, blinking, stillness in the body, flatting out of the facial muscles. All of these were present. I was able to describe them and observe that they had enhanced them.*

*After this experience she was very satisfied and said, "I'll be able to use this." And she did. She was able to have the baby with no medication and with a sense of comfort and satisfaction of looking forward to that baby and not needing to pay attention to anything that she didn't need to pay attention to. She was very pleased with that and so was I.*

People suffering with painful sensations can be relieved to be reminded of this and invited into the possibility of not noticing those unwanted painful sensations.

## NOT BEING BOTHERED

I was intentionally irritated one night when the next-door neighbours were having a noisy party and the music was so loud, it was hard for me to go to sleep. I had to go to work the next day and it irritated me that these annoying people were keeping me awake.

Of course, the more annoyed I became, the louder the music seemed until, at some point, something changed. I realised that I was having a miserable time staying awake, and they were having a party! Somehow that recognition quietened the music in my experience so it was not bothering anywhere near as much and I was able to go to sleep.

A man told me that there was a dog that would make a loud barking noise at 2:00am every morning. And he didn't know what to do. It was such a horrible noise. He said one night he realised it was really rather a weird thought to have, but he found himself thinking, "Isn't it kind of that dog to make this noise as a lullaby so that I could go to sleep?" He started to have the experience of the dog singing a lullaby, which he said sounds crazy, but the noise no longer bothered him and he was able to sleep undisturbed and didn't even notice several months later that the dog had died and that noise wasn't happening.

An Australian Olympic marathon runner, Robert de Castella, was asked in an interview how he could continue in running a marathon when even halfway through the marathon, every muscle in his body is painful. And De Castella, or Deeks, as he was called, quipped, "A bit of pain never hurt anybody."

When I was in general practice, delivering babies and doing other things that general practitioners do, the last 10 deliveries that I was there for were hypnotic deliveries. One of the experiences that these women found so helpful was the idea of looking forward to the next contraction, knowing that the sooner the contraction would come, the stronger the contraction was, the sooner all of the labour would be over and they could hold their baby. So this changed their experience of the pain from something to be avoided or managed to be something that they not only weren't bothered by, but actually anticipated enthusiastically so that the whole process could be over and they could hold their baby.

We all have sensations that we don't need to notice and there are many sensations, which even if we do notice them, we don't need to be bothered by them. These two ways of having a potential influence of a client's response to unwanted stimuli can be so helpful in many experiences. The people who are haunted by voices, critical voices, nasty voices, sometimes even evil voices, usually want the voices gone. So as well as trying to not notice the voices, which often only makes them louder, we can help them to be less bothered by them, so then like any bully, not getting the response they want, they get bored and they can go away.

*One of my sons, when he was about four, woke me one night saying there was a monster trying to harm him. And he was very scared. Every time he went to sleep, this monster was there. So I offered him the idea that a lot of monsters get really annoyed at little boys because they're so scared and they never ask the monster what their name is. I invited him to go to bed, go to sleep and to hope that the monster would be there so he could ask the monster what his name was. I didn't hear any more from him that night and, in the morning, I asked him, "Was the monster there?" "Yes."*

*"Did you ask him his name?" "Yes." "And what happened then?" Then my son said, "After he told me what his name was, I asked him if he'd like a cup of tea." Instead of the nightmare being so awful for him, the monster wasn't bothering him at all. He was just someone to have a cup of tea with.*

## WHICH AND WHEN?

What hypnotic experience is missing that could be part of the solution?

I have introduced these experiences as ordinary, everyday experiences so that with hypnosis they can be more easily available and then extended to provide relief that will be tailored to each individual's needs. This avoids the need for jargon and weirdness, which will only add to the difficulty for all.

When to use which will be informed by the wonderful question "What's missing?" and, if we listen to what a client says or ask specifically what would be helpful, we will hear what will be relevant in each situation.

If someone wants more closeness or more space, then connecting and disconnecting will be called for.

If the solution has something to do with time, let's explore ways of stretching or extending their experience of time.

If their problem calls for resolution of some past event or creating a different future - let's play with hypnotic time traveling.

If pain is severe, not noticing is likely to be useful, or if suffering is the main complaint, then learning not being bothered will be worth exploring.

I trust these reflections will be helpful for your learning so we can add to our effectiveness in relieving suffering and add to our personal satisfaction at the same time.

# SECTION 4
## APPLYING HYPNOSIS CLINICALLY

### AN INTRODUCTION

Although applying hypnosis clinically is going to be the focus and the desired outcome of reading a book such as this, this section, in my view, is the least important. I even wondered about leaving it out entirely, but decided to include it, just for the sake of completion and in case there may be some small additional insights that might follow or some additional options that might result from your reading.

After my time with Erickson, I saw that looking at specific conditions became irrelevant or even troublesome. It becomes increasingly clear that we are never dealing with anxiety, depression, trauma, etc. We are always in conversation with a unique individual that is stuck in an unwanted experience and wanting to move on with their life. As we explored in the second section, this approach provides an exploration with each individual person about what is missing for them and then to explore with them where that resource might be available elsewhere in their experience, in particular, in their likes. And then, by helping them to find and connect with this experience that is missing in their problem, by connecting with it, by learning it, it can be brought to bear on the problem area leading to its total, easy, respectful resolution.

And to recap, we are not interested so much in this approach to find out what is wrong so we can diagnose and treat it. Instead, we are interested to converse as one human being with another and explore with each individual client just what it is that's missing for them that, if they were able to access it, they would be okay. Then, having explored with each individual client their unique experience, to help them connect with this resource.

Because the process allows someone the opportunity to see what's there, right under their nose, so to speak, and had been overlooked, the therapy can often be quite brief, sometimes surprisingly so.

Because this approach emphasises each individual's unique experience, the therapy is experienced as respectful and leading to a lasting resolution.

Sometimes clients will come with a diagnosis. They might say, "I am suffering from anxiety. I'm depressed. I've got OCD. I'm suffering from PTSD. I've got an addictive personality." And if a client comes already with this label, which will relate to what's wrong with them that needs fixing, we can acknowledge that and then help them to connect with what's missing for them. As well as that diagnosis being part of their experience, we can help them find out as well as the diagnosis, parallel to the diagnosis, not instead of the diagnosis, but find out just what their experience is and how they would prefer it to be. So then we can apply the principles of this approach and help to loosen the grip that any diagnosis might still have for them.

*A man was referred to me to have help with his sleeping. His GP had told him that the sleeping problem was a result of him suffering from depression. He said that he felt a huge sense of relief when he was diagnosed as being depressed. "I thought that there was something wrong with me," he said. "But now I know I'm depressed I feel so much better."*

*After acknowledging his diagnosis, we could explore how he might best get out of his depression and also what might be helpful for his sleeping. Not surprisingly, as he began to sleep better, his depression lifted. He asked about his anti-depression medication and we agreed that he would know when he didn't need it any more. Within 3 months, he decided that he could stop them gradually and was additionally relieved to discover that he no longer needed them.*

*My attitude that the diagnosis was unimportant would have been a disrespectful imposition, while his belief, when validated, could be respected, resulting in a good outcome.*

*"The good physician treats the disease; the great physician treats the patient who has the disease"*
*- Sir William Osler*

## PROBLEMS WITH MOODS - ANXIETY AND DEPRESSION

If someone comes with a diagnosis of anxiety, we can assume that as with any fear, there will be some issue about some future loss or damage. The most useful exploration that we can share with the client is to find out what they mean by anxiety. Anxiety, as a word, reveals something, but it also conceals a lot more. And if we can explore with each individual client just what their experience is that they're calling anxiety, we might discover that they're feeling insecure, uncertain, afraid, and unsafe.

When we find out in their words, rather than approach from the therapeutic jargon that anxiety is, this is going to allow us to explore the unique experience that this person is having and help to tailor our approach to this unique person rather than trying to find some overarching standard method of treating anxiety.

If someone comes with a label of depression, in the same way as exploring anxiety, it makes such a beautiful difference to find out what they mean, what their experience is that they're calling depression, and this will vary widely between different individuals.

When we ask, "What is the experience that's happening for you that you're calling depression?" some people will say that they feel sad. Some people are feeling resigned. Others, hopeless, helpless, worthless, grieving. And because all of these different experiences are different with different people, getting some clarity about this will make a huge difference to the mood, to the respectfulness and to the speed and lasting influence of our therapy.

In this way, we're never dealing with anxiety or depression. And, at the risk of sounding like a broken record, we're always having a conversation with the person, helping them to connect with some resource, some experience that is missing for them, which is why they have the problem, the anxiety, the depression as they call it, and which, when they can reconnect with it, they can get on with their life.

As with any diagnosis or with any label that someone comes with, if we try and peel it off, and if you've ever tried to peel a label off something, this will make sense to you, even when the label is removed, some of the glue remains behind. There's some residue. So, instead of trying to talk someone out of suffering from an anxiety state or being clinically depressed, instead of talking them out of that, we can have an exploration with them to help them connect with what will be useful for them so that the diagnoses of anxiety and depression can recede into the background and they can get on with their life.

Another benefit of dealing with each person and their experience is that the person is always having the experience they're having that's troubling them. And if we deal with that, then we don't have to get into conversations of comorbidity. It's popular in clinical writing to read how prevalent it is for someone, who is suffering from anxiety to have a co-morbid condition of depression. If we look at the experience, there is no co-morbidity. All there is, is an experience that is labeled as two distinct, but connected experiences.

When we deal with the experience, we don't have to be side-tracked by these conversations, diagnoses, co-morbidities.

## PROBLEMS WITH PAST TRAUMA

We human beings have all had traumatic experiences in our past, beginning with being born, and for many people, giving birth. Trauma is a part of living and we can't avoid it. In the vast majority of situations, the trauma that happens to us, the loss of a school friend, a fall in the playground, a pet dying, all of these traumas that happen to all of us somehow are resolved spontaneously. And most of them are even forgotten so it's as if they never happened. We may even have learnt by falling over as a child recurrently, to keep our balance.

Whether they are resolved, forgotten or whether we learnt from them, they cease to be problematic.

Sometimes, however, the trauma that happened in the past hangs around in the present in some way and causes suffering, causes some limitations of our options, disturbs us. It's as if some part of the past continues into our present.

When this happens, it's important to remember that each person will have their own unique experience of this. A whole number of people can even be in the same traumatic event and each one have their own unique response. When the event, which is past, is still present to them in some way, some might be haunted by intrusive memories or flashbacks. Others might be troubled by surges of overwhelming emotions, yet others will be restricted in their behaviour so that they might have trouble sleeping, going to work, driving or being in a relationship, to name a few.

Because the way the past trauma is still present will be different for each unique individual, it's going to be so important for us to explore with each individual just what is still troubling them, what is still limiting them, what is still causing suffering in them. And then, instead of treating PTSD according to some rigid protocol, we can explore with each individual, tailor our approach to this individual so that together we can clarify what is missing for them, what it is that will make a difference to them, what will be helpful to them so that they can leave the past in the past and be present and live into their future.

If someone is haunted by intrusive memories or flashbacks, then we can explore how we can forget things that are no longer relevant or we can find a way of creating a ritual so that the past can be completed.

If someone is troubled by overwhelming emotions, we can help them to be less connected with those emotions, more disconnected, as if they're watching something on a television set, on a movie screen from some distance so that they can then be disconnected or at least less connected with the emotion so that it's no longer overwhelming.

If a person is suffering because of a problem with going to sleep, we can work with them to help them to sleep or to go to work or whatever it is that is troubling them, limiting them and all of this can happen without needing, without it being necessary to return to the trauma with the risk of re-traumatising them. And also ,we have the relief of not having to be traumatised vicariously by witnessing or being present to the client's trauma.

*A woman was haunted by memories of her young son, who nearly died, fuelled by his terrifyingly rapid worsening she witnessed on the way to hospital. Several years after he'd made a full recovery, these visions disturbed her peace of mind. It soon became apparent that thinking about the near tragedy triggered memories that interfered with her experience of his present health. She was captured and paralysed by how close she came to losing him. For her, it was as if he was always about to die.*

*In hypnosis, she was invited to recall seeing her son earlier on the day of her session with me and to notice that he was healthy, well and happy. She was able to experience this and after allowing herself to be present to it, and learn it, was able to replace his near death with her present peaceful experience that he was alive! Her fear changes into gratitude.*

*Several years later, the resolution was still solid.*

## PROBLEMS WITH PAIN

Nobody wants to feel pain and yet, without pain, we probably would not have survived as long as we have. Pain can have a signal value, alerting us to the need to do something different - remove our hand from a hot stove, have a broken bone set so it can heal.

Most painful experiences are resolved, but some persist and cause suffering and we are asked to help.

It's helpful to recognise that pain has two components - the sensation itself and the associated response to the sensation.

For some, it's the intensity of the sensations that are problematic, while for others, it's the bothersomeness.

Hypnosis is wonderful as a way to help someone with their unwanted sensations, both by allowing them to not be "hypnotised" by the pain [to focus on it and become absorbed in it] and also by helping someone to learn how to focus and become absorbed in a preferred experience, such as walking in the bush or garden.

Erickson said that we can sit in a chair and not notice the sensation from the seat or the floor. We can wear glasses and not notice the sensation from our ears and nose. He reminded us that we all have a lifetime of experience of not noticing sensations that are noticeable and so, invites the possibility of not noticing sensations that are not helpful.

We know about people who don't hear busy traffic or planes landing after they have lived near a busy road or airport. It's as if we learn to block the sounds out or not notice them at all.

Hypnosis is also wonderful as a way of helping someone suffering from pain by learning to have a different and preferred response to the sensations - to be less frightened, less opposing, and more accepting and so reduce or even dissolve the suffering element.

Joseph Barber made an astounding and expansive claim that in his experience, all pain is mutable. He emphasised all pain. All pain! Such a beautiful possibility and one we can enjoy learning to explore.

## PROBLEMS WITH HABITS

When we first go public and let others know that we are including hypnosis in our practice, the most common comments are, "Can you help me to stop smoking?" "Can you help me to lose weight?" as if this is the main relevance of hypnosis.

We all develop habits - driving on one side of the road or another, depending where we live on the planet. We move the food from our plate to our mouth without poking our eye out or putting it into our ear.

Like all of our human experiences, these habits can be useful or cause suffering. It's the unwanted habits that bring some people to therapy and require our exploration to be of most use to help clients learn a preferred habit.

Erickson said that all problems are learnt limitations and pointed our attention to the possibility of learning a preferred habit or unlearning a troublesome one. If someone has learnt the habit of smoking cigarettes, they can learn the habit of breathing fresh air. If someone has learnt the habit of being angry, they can learn the habit of being calm or accepting.

After Erickson, we can see the benefit that hypnosis offers as a way of enhancing any learning that is useful.

In this approach, then, we are going to be less interested in applying some set protocol of stopping smoking, losing weight, etc., and more interested in exploring how each individual is experiencing their habit, what specifically is problematic about it, what's missing for them so it can be resolved.

This results in greater effectiveness, more respectful outcomes, and more satisfaction and enjoyment for us. Everyone benefits!

## PROBLEMS WITH OBSESSIONS AND COMPULSIONS

We can think of an obsession as an unwanted thought that gets stuck, and a compulsion as an unwanted behaviour that takes us over so we have no control over it.

Anyone can develop an obsession simply by trying not to think of it - don't think of a pink elephant right now and we are in danger of being trampled to death by a herd of elephants. It is as if the unwanted thought "hypnotises" us and fills our awareness. Hypnosis can help to play with the thought and have more freedom around it so that it becomes "just a thought" or disappears completely, just as a bully loses interest when we don't play their game.

Compulsions can "hypnotise" us [we become focussed and absorbed in the unwanted behaviour] so we can then help someone to "come out of trance" so they are no longer "hypnotised" by the compulsion or we can invite such a person into a preferred experience that they can focus on and become absorbed in.

*A trainee nurse asked for help with her weight. She said the problem was the caramel custards in the cafeteria. Each morning, about 11am, they started calling her and she couldn't resist them. She asked for hypnosis to help her get over her compulsion. I offered her the idea that she didn't need to be hypnotised by me, rather, she could learn how to not be hypnotised by the caramel custards. Since it was approaching 11.30 am, I invited her to go to the cafeteria, look the camel custards in the eye, and see if she could hypnotise them before they hypnotised her. A week later she let me know that the caramel custards were very hypnotically responsive.*

Rather than treating OCD, we can explore what's missing for each individual and assist them to find it and learn it - yet one more example of connecting an individual human being with their resourcefulness rather than treating a condition.

## WORKING WITH CHILDREN

Some therapists are reluctant to work with children, assuming that they are difficult or different. I have found that the same principles apply and because they have not been as socialised as we adults. They are a lot more open, flexible and creative. My experience is that they are much easier to work with.

Instead of some complex, convoluted invitation into trance, all we need to do is ask if they would like to play a game, to pretend or imagine something. They might like to watch their favourite TV show, play their favourite computer game, read their favourite book. Then we are up and running with no fuss, no doubts, no concerns.

I was asked to run workshop in Copenhagen 10 years ago for therapists wanting to use hypnosis with children. The 15 or so therapists, all adults, had fun imagining that they were children, and we had some very useful playful learning.

One of Erickson's characteristic stories, particularly in his latter years, was to speak about early learning. "When you first learnt to walk …" "When you first learnt the letters of the alphabet …" These early learning stories help to have us connect with our younger, more flexible, more willing selves and so contribute to the ease and effectiveness of our learning to heal.

*An 11 year old girl had a dog phobia, liked reading a fantasy book "Pigs Might Fly," running and fractions. I asked her if we could play and she willingly agreed. She found that closing her eyes was helpful for her imagining and we created a variation on the theme of the book she was ready where a little girl was in "the wrong land" and was going to find her way back home. She readily accepted the idea that in "the way, wrong land" the little girl could be frightened of dogs but when she arrived home, there would be a dog there that she could enjoy patting. She was then willing to begin to run towards home [she said she liked running] and to let me know when she was 1/2 way, 3/4 way then 7/8 of the way home [she liked fractions] and then when she arrived home there was the dog, and she enjoyed patting it. This conversation lasted less than 30 minutes. Several months later, she had a dog. And when I followed up 10 years later, she still had the same dog, and had no sign of her previous phobia.*

*A 9 year old girl had been having nightmares about sharks for three months. She told me that she was enjoying reading Harry Potter. She was more than willing to play a game, so when I asked her to imagine that she was Harry Potter's sister, a wizard and not a muggle, she smiled. In response to my invitation to take out her wand and make a spell that would protect her from the sharks, her smile widened. She said she had just surrounded herself with a white light. When I challenged her about the power of the spell, she brought the sharks in, said they were getting frustrated because they couldn't bite through the white light, now they were getting bored, now they were swimming away. After that brief conversation of about 15 minutes, she had no further nightmares.*

## PROBLEMS WITH RELATIONSHIPS

We humans are relating beings. Our relationships are the major source of joy and our pain.

Couples come to us because of some dissatisfaction or conflict and, if we ask them what the problem is, they usually show us with a few moments ... "He ..." "She ...," etc. It's enough to see their partner or even think about them, and the conflict is in full view. It is as if each "hypnotises" the other into a "bad trance."

No wonder some therapists are reluctant to work with couples because they say that it's difficult enough working with one person, but two ...!!!

I have found that if we approach a couple as an entity, then any approach we use with an individual can be translated into working with a couple. We can ask an individual, and hence the couple, "What do you like to do as a couple?" "What is the problem for you as a couple that you want to have some help with?" "What's missing for you as a couple that if you could have it, you'd be OK as a couple?"

These questions avoid being diverted by conversations with two individuals where we can find ourselves cast as judge and jury, where nobody wins and everybody suffers. The responses to these questions, just as with individuals, helps to shift their experience from problem to solution, from stuckness to movement, from suffering and discord to peace and satisfaction.

Also, if we invite a couple into hypnosis together, they then have a shared experience which can be pleasing and can be the beginning of discovering other shared experience that can be pleasing.

The result of this approach is often a complete resolution and even a transformation where, instead of two individuals having to accept a compromise, they can each and both have the pleasure of a shared resolution with shared satisfaction.

*A couple travelled from interstate for a resolution to their escalating conflict. When I asked them what they liked to do as a couple, they looked at each other with puzzled faces before they each began to recall that they used to go out for dinner and see a movie and they hadn't been doing this because of work pressure. I asked them what their plans were for that night and, since they were away from home, they had already planned to have dinner together and wondered about seeing a movie! The mood in the room was palpably different - lighter and more peaceful - and as they left, they were looking forward to the evening. There was no conflict in the air. I didn't see them again, so I don't know about the long-term effects, but it was clear to all of us that something was different and the possibility of relating again was real for the first time in a while.*

## GROUP HYPNOSIS

As with couples, we can approach a group as an entity and assist them to have a shared experience, which can be so helpful for creating a mood of trust, openness and cohesion - to literally create a group where there was previously a gathering of individuals.

I have found it to be very helpful to keep my language general, to offer multiple alternatives, to be as inclusive and permissive as possible so that no-one is alienated and disconnected from the experience. For example, I might say, *"Everyone has their own way of focusing and becoming absorbed, so you can find your own way of finding yourself having the experience that is useful for you, not what you think I want you to have, not what you think you want to have, but the experience that will be useful for you, and just for you."*

By using inclusive language, anyone in the group can respond to the invitation individually and feel respected with no force or obligation.

We can easily tailor the experience when we know what the shared concerns are for a group. If the group consists of people recovering from trauma or loss, we can explore with them what might be missing - healing, recovering, learning … whatever might emerge as we explore - and then all we need to do is to offer as many alternatives as possible - *"This can happen now or later; with awareness or by surprise; slowly or rapidly; intermittently at first or permanently,"* etc. The more alternatives we offer, the more likely it is that at least one will be acceptable.

It's also helpful to offer as many ways of responding as possible, so no one is excluded, and all are included. *"You can listen to me, or my words, or the sound of my voice, or you can let your mind wander; you can translate anything I say into words that are meaningful to you; I can't know how best to speak to you, since I know so little about you, but you know more about you than you realise,"* etc.

The creation of a shared experience can be a wonderful way to create a group coherence as well as a mood of mutual trust and support.

## SELF HYPNOSIS

When we first drive a different car, visit a different city, live in a different house, it can take some time to learn where the ignition key goes, where the train station is, where the light switches are and, as we learn, the ignition key, the railway station, the light switches become transparent.

Once someone has experienced hypnosis, we can simply ask them to remember the experience and with minimal encouragement help them to find their way back to a previous hypnotic experience.

It can be that easy, that simple, with no need for any formal protocol or "post-hypnotic suggestion," simply an opportunity for anyone interested to remember, re-experience, and learn in their own way.

*We can ask someone how they like to go into hypnosis and invite this experience to emerge. And then, once someone is in trance, we can ask them to come out of trance, then we can ask them how they might recall that experience and as they do, to encourage their experience by saying, "That's good; that's right; your eyes are ...; your breathing is ...; your face is smoothing out ..." anything that indicates an increased focus and absorption and then remind them that learning anything is helped by familiarity. "Each time you recall this experience, it will be easier to find it."*

## A DISCLAIMER

Every aspect of what is included here has been about easy. My experience of using and teaching hypnosis over the last four decades is that if we can make an easy start and do what we can to make the process as easy as we can for each client, then everyone benefits. Instead of overwhelm, lack of self-confidence and the killer mood of resignation, we can have a place to begin from, a genuine self-confidence, and the enlivening mood of possibility.

Obviously not everyone is going to be easy, not everyone is going to progress easily. It would be naive to think so.

However, I've found, and have had recurrent reports from others that starting easy and expecting an easy process seems to skew the outcome towards easy.

That is why I'm not recommending this approach, simply inviting you to explore and discover for yourself.

Thank you for being willing to explore with me.

*"Many scholars have made the Buddha's teaching complicated and difficult to understand. But the Buddha said things very simply and did not get caught up in words. So if a teaching is too complicated, it is not the sound of the Buddha."*
- *Thich Nhat Hanh*

*"Gentlemen, I have a confession to make. Half of what we have taught you is in error and furthermore, we cannot tell you which half it is."*

*- Sir William Osler*

# About The Author

Robert McNeilly was in general medical practice for 10 years, conducted a private hypnotherapy practice for 25 years, and after meeting Milton H Erickson in USA, began teaching diploma courses in counselling and hypnosis with a solution orientation to interested health workers nationally and internationally.

He has authored another 4 books - "Healing with Words" with Jenny Brown and "Healing the Whole Person" published by Wiley, recently republished as "Doing Change - conversations for moving on" by St Luke's Innovative Resources and Creating Connections Vol 1 & 2 with Tandava Press. He has also published a number of eBooks with Amazon Kindle.

Robert B McNeilly MBBS
Director, The Centre of Effective Therapy
Co-director, The Milton H Erickson Institute of Tasmania
191 Campbell Street
Hobart TAS 7000
Australia
email rob@cet.net.au
www.cet.net.au